Releasing Healing

Steven J. Anderson

Published by Healing Rooms Scotland, P O Box 7010, Glasgow G76 0WF United Kingdom. Telephone 0044 (0)141 637 4445.

www.healingrooms-scotland.com

Printed in the United Kingdom   ISBN 978-0-9562397-0-9

Endorsement:

"I've known Steven and worked with him for many years as a colleague in ministry in the city of Glasgow. It has been thrilling to see the development of his ministry as he has stepped out in faith and grown in understanding and experience of the vital part the healing ministry must have in the witness of the church in the west today. I warmly commend this book because it is so thoroughly Biblical and full of down-to-earth practical guidelines. It also tackles honestly some of the difficult questions raised about healing today. I personally found it very helpful, full of hope and challenge." Edwin Gunn, former Senior Pastor, Queen's Park Baptist Church, Glasgow (now retired)

Contents

Introduction   4

1. Everything is Possible   9

2. The Difficult Questions   20

3. Creating a Healing Environment   42

4. Going Deeper: Healing Damaged Lives   66

5. Healing as a Sign and a Wonder   91

6. An Explosion of the Miraculous   105

7. Appointed and Anointed to be Fruitful   118

8. Living in the Spirit of Generosity   135

9. Stretch and Build   144

Appendix 1: An Overview of Healing in the Bible

Appendix 2: God's Prescription for Health

Appendix 3: Proverbs for Healing and Life

Introduction

Many people have a decade or a period in their lives, which made a deep and formative impact upon them. The 1980's were such a time for me. As a young man at the start of that decade, I fell in love with two people – Helen who soon became my wife, and Jesus Christ who has become my constant companion, my friend, my inspiration, my Lord and my God, who gives eternal significance to all I do.

Our lives sped forward through the next few years through several highs and lows, feeling at times like a wild water ride, throwing up challenges and thrills. The first great challenge came in 1983. After just over a year of married life, I responded to what I sensed was God's call to pastoral ministry, and was accepted to train at the Baptist College in Glasgow. At the same time our first son was born, which all seems good so far. However, within days, Helen had sunk into deep post-natal depression, and over the next weeks and months, we experienced times of great anguish and pain. The doctors gave little hope of any recovery for a long time; one psychiatrist describing Helen's condition as one of the deepest depressions he had ever seen. Everything seemed dark and bleak. However, many people were praying. After five months of this darkness God spoke. It was the middle of the night as Helen sat up feeding our son, staring blankly, feeling so little emotion or anything else, that the voice of the Lord spoke. One word and that was it. Helen 'heard' the Lord saying 'enough!' It was a still small voice into her inner being, but a mighty voice that thundered into the depth of that depression. Immediately the lights went on and everything was different. Helen has never suffered a day of depression in her life since.

In the next years, we had to deal with untimely deaths in our families with both of us losing brothers in their twenties. Yet through all this, our testimony was God is good and his love endures forever. Indeed, it was often through the most difficult times that I can look back and see the greatest times of character development, and preparation of my life for all that God would lead me into in the years ahead.

The eighties also brought some very different experiences. It was in 1985 that I went to a conference in the south of England, where the late John Wimber was speaking about the Kingdom of God. Not only did I have my mind opened to new understandings, but also my life was impacted hugely by a powerful experience of the Holy Spirit, releasing and launching me into new areas of gifting and ministry.

Soon after this, I became the pastor of a small Baptist church on a large housing estate in Glasgow. The following years contained similar highs and lows, but through it all, we began to pray for the sick, and see numbers of people set free from demonic bondage in their lives. Noticeably, we witnessed a far higher percentage of healing take place when we ministered to people who were not in the church.

I guess much was formed in me through that time that continues to make me who I am in Christ. As I now focus much of my time on the areas of healing the sick and setting free the oppressed I continue to face certain challenges, and hear of the challenges and questions that many sincere people have in regard to healing. This book is an attempt to bring some Biblical and practical understanding to these challenges. It is also written to be an encouragement to the whole Body of Christ, every follower of Jesus, to follow him fully and to do what he did. A significant part of that is to release healing into our communities in his name as a sign of his kingdom.

I want to bring some understanding, not give easy, simplistic answers or make glib statements. I will address the questions I am often asked, or have to face:

What about those people who don't appear to get healed?
Why if Jesus healed so many have we seen so few being healed?
Is it all a matter of faith?
If so, why are folks who do not believe in Jesus healed?
Why do some people appear to be made well only to get sick again?

These are just some of the questions you may have. I hope that this book may bring some fresh light, insight and hope to you.

Releasing Healing In Jesus Name

The purpose of this book is to encourage and equip the church to release healing in our world, giving healing ministry its proper emphasis as a key means of reaching our communities with the Good News of the Kingdom.

We need to release healing in the following areas:

1. **From misconceptions.**
There have been many misconceptions about healing; from those who concluded it was only for New Testament times and therefore does not happen today; to those who have dismissed the miraculous altogether, 'demythologising' Jesus' healings and miracles; to those who have not experienced healing through prayer, and concluded that God does not want to heal them; to talk of thorns in the flesh, and much more.

2. **From hindrances and roadblocks.**
Isaiah 57:14 says to remove the obstacles out of the way of my people. We must understand that there are many things on earth, and in our lives, that block the grace of God. Unforgiveness towards those who have wronged us is one of the most common. These matters will be discussed more fully in chapter 2.

3. **As a sign of the Kingdom of God.**
How we need to grasp this – the primary purpose of healing is not for the church, but for those who do not yet believe. Healing is to be a sign pointing the way and a wonder making people reflect on who Jesus is in whose name they have just

experienced healing. Chapter 5 will focus on this matter.

4. **From heaven to earth**.

The heart of the prayer that Jesus taught us is *'Let your kingdom come, let your will be done, on earth as it is in heaven.'* It is releasing what is in heaven onto the earth. Bill Johnson has written much on this, and I wholeheartedly recommend his books wherever I go. Many in the church need to re-direct their focus from getting off earth into heaven, to primarily getting what is in heaven onto the earth.

Our focus can so often be hooked into the problems of life around us. This can lead to discouragement, and even hopelessness. Our perspective can so easily become a negative and even cynical one. I believe the Holy Spirit wants to renew our minds and our vision. Let us begin to look at the possibilities that Jesus wants to introduce us to.

Chapter 1
Everything is Possible

Everything is possible for him who believes. Mark 9:23

A woman visited one of our Healing Rooms who had been diagnosed with cervical cancer. After receiving ministry of prayer for healing, she felt well, and the nausea and sickness that had troubled her for some time stopped. When she returned to the hospital for a further examination there was no trace of cancer, and more than that, the doctor told her that it looked like she had been given a brand new cervix!

From many places, we hear reports of phenomenal healings – missing body parts appearing, blind eyes opening, even the dead being raised. Some rejoice, but some are sceptical. Some believe these things may happen elsewhere, but have no expectancy for such wonders to occur in their life, or their church or town. Yet we should ask as Peter did after the lame man was healed: *'why does this surprise you'* (Acts 3:12). If we believe in God – the Creator, the Almighty – then surely nothing is too hard, and everything is a possibility. If we believe in Jesus – the Resurrection and the Life – then surely he can do all things.

However, there are things that can happen that interfere with our faith and that can crush our expectancy. In Mark chapter 9 a man brings his son to Jesus' disciples in the hope that they will cast a demon out of him, thus setting him free and healing him. When Jesus arrives on the scene, having been up the mountain with Peter, James and John, he finds the remaining disciples locked in argument with the religious rulers. The reason for the situation of contention was due to the inability of those disciples to drive out the demon. Indeed a powerless church will often find itself reduced to arguments.

Jesus enters the arena and everything changes. We will come to this story again in chapter two, but for now, we see that this father's faith was, at first, severely dented by the ineffectiveness of the disciples. Likewise, our experience can tell us not to expect too much; that we just have to live with certain conditions, and even oppressive circumstances. Some caution us not to be too expectant for fear that we will be disappointed. In all this, we pull the revelation of the Scriptures down to the level of our experience. We must not do this. We must not let our past experience dictate our present expectation, but let the revelation of the Word of God lead to true expectation. We must let Jesus speak his words that are spirit and are life: *'everything is possible to him who believes.'*

On another occasion, Jesus encounters what appears to be a hopeless situation. In Luke 8:41 he comes across Jairus, a synagogue ruler. This man is desperate; his young daughter lies at home dying. Before Jesus can get to his house, a messenger arrives with the news that Jairus dreaded: *'your daughter is dead.'* All hope is gone. It is over. It is too late. Jesus responds with words that could have sounded ridiculous and even cruel: *'don't be afraid; just believe.'*

Fear is one of the most powerful forces affecting our lives. As we minister healing to many people, repeatedly we come across the grip of fear deep in the human soul. Lives can be ruled by fear – fear of failure, fear of loss, fear of illness, fear of rejection, fear of the future and fear of just about anything, even fear of fear! If we allow fear to rule over us, it can destroy us. Jesus came to bring life, to bring freedom, and to bring the love of the Father. *There is no fear in love. But perfect love drives out fear.* (1 John 4:18)

Fear and its companion intimidation come in when the problem looks bigger than the solution. If you owe a bill of £200, but only have £100, you might fear that you cannot pay the bill. If you are diagnosed with a disease that you are told there is no effective cure for, then you fear the disease will take its toll, as it appears greater than any cure.

Jesus words came blasting into Jairus' ears to counter the onset of fear. His words of course would be meaningless unless he can back them up in action. He does just that bringing the girl back to life. His words have true substance. Whatever we face, his word to us is not to give in to fear for he has overcome all our enemies, including the ultimate enemy of death.
Death has been swallowed up in victory. (1 Cor. 15:54)

The second part of what Jesus says to Jairus is *'just believe.'* However, how can he? He has just heard his precious daughter is dead. How easy is it just to believe, just to trust the Lord? It is easy to say, and some people say it glibly. Nevertheless, it is true that God is good and he can be trusted. We need to take him at his word sometimes with a simple, yet profound, faith.

An elderly woman called Dolly came into one of our Healing Rooms one afternoon. Her legs were bandaged, and she told us that she had ulcers affecting both legs so badly that she was waiting to have them surgically removed. Dolly had a simple and profound faith, and told us that we would pray, and Jesus would heal her. We duly obeyed, and off she went. I got a letter a few days later saying that Dolly had been to her doctor later on, and told him she had received prayer and God had healed her. The doctor, maybe somewhat sceptically, said to her that he would remove the bandages and then they would see. He took the bandages off both legs, but could not find one trace of an ulcer on either leg!

Everything is possible because Jesus has triumphed. That is not a statement of unfounded optimism or triumphalism. It is the Word of God: "Behold, the Lion of the tribe of Judah, the Root of David, has triumphed." (Revelation 5:5)

He has triumphed, and now he seeks to invade our lives and our world with the enforcement of his victory. That does not mean all our problems vanish like with the wave of a wand. It means he invites us into a partnership and process of transformation and new creation. He invites us to believe, to respond, actively to receive and to act, to start living in a new way, with a new mindset. His priority is to transform us that we might be agents of transformation bringing his Kingdom on earth.

As he raised the young girl back to life, so he wants to bring to life our hopes and dreams. He wants us to dream with him of what could be, of the possibilities of this time. We have begun to see something, maybe the cloud the size of a man's hand, and there is much more to come.

Can we dream and believe to see the incurable cured in Jesus name; to see people healed from the torments of mental disturbance; to see cancers bow to Jesus name; to see depressions lift at his command? Can we dream and believe to see transformation breaking out into broken families who have been ravaged by all manner of harm? Can we dream and believe to see communities turned around as the power of Christ's words and Spirit breaks in with a new level of impact?

Jesus entered Jerusalem on what we call Palm Sunday riding on a donkey. Matthew 21:10 says, "When Jesus entered Jerusalem, the whole city was stirred and asked 'Who is this?'" Could it be possible that through his present Body on earth that Jesus could again enter cities causing such a stir that everyone is asking who he is?

As the part of our life story that I shared in the introduction shows, Helen and I have not been unacquainted with difficulties. What I hope we are learning is that where life brings pain God brings possibility; that when we admit to human failure we can take hold of faith in God; and that difficulties and despair can lead us into a desperation that drives us into the heart of God, finding his solution is greater than the problem. We have an enemy who seeks to bring intimidation and limitation into our lives. Just as Goliath stood intimidating the armies of Israel who drew back in fear, so the enemy seeks to make us draw back from fulfilling the purposes of God in our time. However, just as a young shepherd boy called David refused to give in to fear, simply believed, and so slew Goliath, we can do likewise today. The Israelites looked at the sheer size and presence of Goliath in relation to themselves; David looked at the smallness and weakness of the arrogant Philistine in relation to his God.

If intimidation is allowed to do its work then it produces limitation. That is the enemy's goal. The church has been far too intimidated, and consequently allowed itself to be limited way below what God said she could do.

It is time to get a proper perspective, and to see from the heavenly standpoint. To see as Elisha's servant did, that those who are for us far outnumber those who are against us. It is time to cast off the threatening giants of intimidation, and cut loose from the deceptive weights of limitation. It is time to soar with the Holy Spirit whom Jesus gives to us without limit (John 3:34). It is time to believe Jesus no matter what screams at us to the contrary. It is time to enter the field of possibilities where we will see the Kingdom of God come with power.

When faced with the first wave of opposition and persecution the early believers gathered together and prayed:

Now, Lord, consider their threats and enable your servants to speak your word with great boldness. Stretch out your hand to heal and perform miraculous signs and wonders through the name of your holy servant Jesus. (Acts 4:29-30)

The River of Life and Healing
The man brought me back to the entrance of the temple, and I saw water coming out from under the threshold of the temple toward the east (for the temple faced east). The water was coming down from under the south side of the temple, south of the altar. He then brought me out through the north gate and led me around the outside to the outer gate facing east, and the water was flowing from the south side. As the man went eastward with a measuring line in his hand, he measured off a thousand cubits and then led me through water that was ankle-deep. He measured off another thousand cubits and led me through water that was knee-deep. He measured off another thousand and led me through water that was up to the waist. He measured off another thousand, but now it was a river that I could not cross, because the water had risen and was deep enough to swim in—a river that no one could cross. He asked me, "Son of man, do you see

this?"

Then he led me back to the bank of the river. When I arrived there, I saw a great number of trees on each side of the river. He said to me, "This water flows toward the eastern region and goes down into the Arabah, where it enters the Sea. When it empties into the Sea, the water there becomes fresh. Swarms of living creatures will live wherever the river flows. There will be large numbers of fish, because this water flows there and makes the salt water fresh; so where the river flows everything will live. Fishermen will stand along the shore; from En Gedi to En Eglaim there will be places for spreading nets. The fish will be of many kinds—like the fish of the Great Sea. But the swamps and marshes will not become fresh; they will be left for salt. Fruit trees of all kinds will grow on both banks of the river. Their leaves will not wither, nor will their fruit fail. Every month they will bear, because the water from the sanctuary flows to them. Their fruit will serve for food and their leaves for healing. (Ezekiel 47:1-12)

This amazing passage of Scripture, describing the vision Ezekiel was shown, has been speaking powerfully to us in the church in these times. God has been pouring out refreshing waters on his people in response to the many prayers for a renewing of the church and an awakening in our nations. It is important that we understand the fuller implications of what these words are conveying, and that we run with the full measure of what the Spirit of God is doing and calling us to share in with him at this time. This is a vision of what can be and indeed is becoming a reality.

'Where the river flows everything will live' *(v9)*. The Hebrew word *chayah* translated as *live* means to be revived, to be quickened, restored to health, and to prosper in life. Wherever the river flows it brings this wonderful life, the life in all its fullness that Jesus promised (John 10:10).

So what is this river, and where does it come from? It is the very life and breath of God, the Holy Spirit, and it flows from within the house of God, the Temple (v1). We, as followers of and believers in Jesus, are the temple of the Holy Spirit (1 Corinthians 6:19). From within us flow streams of living water (John 7:37-38). These streams combine together, and along with the outpouring of God's Spirit from the heavens form this mighty river. It is not enough to pray for revival and leave it all up to God. We need to co-operate in the co-mission he has called us into with him. As we pray and realise what we carry inside us – the living, dynamic presence of the Holy Spirit - and let this loose, we will see the river of life increasing in depth, bringing life and healing all over the land. Many of the riverbeds in the Western world are dry and only experiencing a trickle of what is available and possible. It is time to see a breaking forth of the water of life.

We notice from these verses that the river gets deeper the further away it travels from the source. There are four different depths measured out just like the four stages Jesus mentions in Acts 1:8 – Jerusalem, Judea, Samaria and to the ends of the earth. Now it is vital we remain close and connected to the source, but it is equally important that we flow out carrying God's presence into the uttermost and darkest parts of the earth. As we go in obedience to the command of Jesus we will experience a deepening of his anointing on us.

Ezekiel is asked in verse 6, 'do you see this?' God asks us what we see. Are we observant to what he is doing, to the stirrings and activities of the Holy Spirit around us? Are we seeing the first fruits of the harvest that he is surely bringing to our nations?

What else do we notice in this passage? There are many trees and many fish. The trees (v7) grow on each side of the river. These may represent the various churches and ministries that God is working through, and will move through. They are not all the same, and are on different sides of the river, seeing things from a different viewpoint, but all are equally valid and important. The trees are again mentioned in verse 12 where we see that they do not wither, that they bear fruit every month and that their leaves provide healing. They do not wither because they are rooted in Christ and drawing from the river of the Spirit. They do not just bear fruit in season (see Psalm 1:3), but do so continuously. We have often talked of a season for this and a season for that, but now is not just a season for fruitfulness, it is time for a continuous sowing and reaping in God's harvest field.

As the water flows, it literally heals the 'dead' waters, causing the number of fish to abound. This is what can happen in our nations as we let the river loose and do not hold back. There are some areas though (v11) that are not affected. Even in the greatest moves of God, where so many seemingly obvious miraculous events take place, there are still those who refuse to see and believe. As the river flows out into the world, one danger is that there may be some areas of the church that refuse to receive the river, and remain totally unaffected by it.

Our world is hungry for spiritual reality and in need of great healing. The trees – the various expressions of the Body of Christ – have the potential to produce fruit that will truly satisfy that hunger, bringing people into a genuine encounter with God, and to grow the leaves of healing that will cure the many maladies of minds, hearts, bodies and even nations. The key for such trees to grow and produce is that they dwell in this wonderful river of God that brings life wherever it goes. The river of God – the Holy Spirit poured out on us and flowing through us – means *everything is possible to him who believes.* We need to truly believe and understand the incredible potential that we have as carriers of the presence of Christ, and release the activity of his Spirit bringing life, healing and freedom wherever we go.

Chapter 2
The Difficult Questions

I brought him to your disciples, but they could not heal him. Matthew 17:16

Healing the sick was clearly a major thrust of Jesus' ministry.

Great crowds came to him, bringing the lame, the blind, the crippled, the mute and many others, and laid them at his feet; and he healed them. The people were amazed when they saw the mute speaking, the crippled made well, the lame walking and the blind seeing. And they praised the God of Israel. Matthew 15:30-31

Healing is part of the salvation package that Jesus bought for us. The Greek term for salvation - *sozo* - means to save, heal, deliver and rescue. It is translated in various ways including healed, made well or made whole. God is not unwilling to heal, and certainly is able. The real problem with healing lies with the church – primarily our unbelief, but also our lack of understanding to address the blockages to healing. Instead of seeking to justify a lack of healing, we need to seek to grow in faith, understanding and the power of God. We need to do this because it is Biblical, and because healing is a sign to those who do not yet know Christ that his Kingdom is among them and pointing them to faith in him. Healing and miracles were the great evangelistic tools of the church in Acts and we need to recover this focus more fully today.

Jesus gave his church power and authority, and a commission to heal the sick as part of the proclamation and demonstration of the Gospel. A powerless church is a total contradiction to what Jesus modelled and permitted for his Body. As the Body of Christ representing him on earth, we are to be like him. He did not give the sick and oppressed sympathy – he had compassion on them that moved him to do something for them, to heal them and set them free.

There are of course many different views about healing, and there are some important questions that many are looking for good answers to, rather than being fobbed off with dismissive statements. In this chapter I want to give some understanding to the questions people have, and call us to align our thinking with Scripture, and not to base it only on our past and present experiences. Our answer must not be simply to explain why we do not see more healing. Our answer must be one that indicates how we can see more healing.

Some of the positions and understandings about healing today would be as follows: (this is putting it very simply)

1. Healing is in the atonement. That is Christ's death which made us 'at one' with God, not only brings forgiveness of sins but also healing for our bodies (see Isaiah 53:4). Some would say

that this being the case we only need to believe and receive our healing.

2. God does not heal today – healing, miracles, and the gifts of the Spirit were only for the early church in its formative years in the time of the original apostles.

3. God never did miracles – the stories of healings and miracles in the Bible are simply myths designed to teach us some truth.

4. God does heal today, but we should not expect this too often. Those who take this position often point to John 5 where Jesus heals one man at the pool where many sick were gathered, then comments in verse 19 that 'he only does what he sees the Father doing.'

I am aware there are other positions, and those who hold to some of the above will have various understandings about healing within that position. I imagine those who hold to positions 2 and 3 above are not too likely to be reading this book. I believe the first position mentioned above is true, but in its simplest form, fails to take account of the many obstacles that block healing, and that need to be properly addressed, which I will come to in this chapter. My main concern is to address those who would in some way associate with the fourth position. This would include many people who I know and admire.

I believe we must take full account of the weight of what Scripture says about healing letting that form a Biblical expectancy in us, rather than taking our experience to Scripture and seeking to make sense of

Scripture in the light of our experience. Do we bring the Word of God into line with our experience (as many have sought to do over the centuries), or do we seek to bring our experience into line with the Word of God?

As we look at the weight of what the Bible says about healing, I believe that the overwhelming evidence is that God is the Lord who heals (Exodus 15:26), and that Jesus - who shows us most fully what God is like – commonly healed all who came to him. Yes, John 5 may indicate that on one occasion, he healed one man among many infirm people, but we cannot base our understanding on one passage while ignoring the many occasions that show Jesus healing multitudes. In addition, on this occasion, Jesus initiated the conversation and healing; he did not deny or turn away any who sought him. The New Testament church seemed to have a clear expectation of healing for the sick.

Is any one of you sick? He should call the elders of the church to pray over him and anoint him with oil in the name of the Lord. And the prayer offered in faith will make the sick person well; the Lord will raise him up (James 5:14-15a).

Another popular understanding which I have much agreement with, is the concept of the Kingdom of God being present but also being future – it is the now but not yet Kingdom. This is essentially true, but must not be made as an excuse for people not being healed. If the Kingdom broke in among us through the coming of

Jesus, then it is advancing and needs to increase. The increase of his government (Kingdom rule) knows no end (see Isaiah 9:7). The Kingdom is not yet fully here on earth, but our concern is not to explain our lack of healing and so forth through that, but to pray his Kingdom down – your Kingdom come – and work towards the continual increase of his Kingdom.

Sometimes this view concerning the now and not yet of the Kingdom is expressed in its relation to healing as if it is a rather arbitrary matter – some get healed and some do not. This is like the weather forecast telling us there is a 40% risk of showers, so you might catch one but you might not. This will not do, as this thinking ignores the whole area of our responsibility in releasing healing and the question of blockages to healing that can be removed.

All that being said, there are numerous questions and struggles with regard to healing, on which I shall now seek to shed some light.

When we minister to those who come to us, there are several outcomes:

1. Some people do receive instant healing. We see this many times in our Healing Rooms, like someone who came in suffering from ulcerative colitis with even her clothes touching her body causing her pain. After a very short prayer session, the woman left pressing her hand against what had been the painful parts of her body, but now experiencing absolutely no pain.

2. Some people receive healing later on or after a few days. In Luke 17 where Jesus encounters ten lepers, it says in verse 14 that 'as they went they were cleansed.' We have had numerous reports later on of those who felt no healing or freedom from symptoms at the time, but later that day or night experienced complete release and healing.

3. Some people are healed gradually over a period of time and several prayer sessions. This is often the case where healing is a process that may involve the steady building of faith, or time to deal with blockages that are preventing healing, or simply that we need to persevere. After all, even Jesus touched a blind man twice before he could see clearly (Mark 8:22-26).

4. Some people are not healed physically, but are helped in other ways. Some have not experienced healing for the physical condition they may have come for; yet often testify that it was good that they came as they have found peace, strength and other benefits. On saying this, I do not believe we should settle for that, but should be pursuing greater effectiveness in ministering the healing power of Christ to everyone who comes to us.

So how do we answer the questions people have about healing? These may be genuine concerns of both those who are sick, and especially of those with pastoral responsibility in the churches. The biggest concerns seem to be around the possible damaging effects on those who do not appear to be healed. This centres on how the sick perceive themselves in relation to God: "If I am not healed, but someone else is, does that mean that God loves them more?" If I am not healed is it my fault? Am I lacking faith or in sin?" Drawing the wrong conclusions can of course heap guilt on a person, but it is quite unnecessary to fall into this trap. In the next chapter, I shall outline a good practice for healing ministry, which will help to counter some of the bad experiences people may have had.

Wrong Assumptions and Conclusions

I believe we can miss out on what God is doing and saying by moving too quickly in our own understanding, making misguided assumptions and drawing faulty conclusions to what we experience, or indeed do not experience. For example, I have often heard people conclude that God does not want to heal them, that he has a purpose in their sickness, and to back this up they may well point to those who have shown great character and achievement while suffering from some manner of infirmity. Yet I believe that almost all those who say this still take the medication that has been given to help alleviate their suffering, and if offered a medical cure tomorrow would accept it gratefully.

Others have pointed to Scriptures such as James 1:2, which call us to rejoice in trials. But does the text here refer to sicknesses? I doubt it very much. For the New Testament church, the trials were most often persecution, but the Western church today, which knows so little of this, has often, and wrongly, substituted sickness for the trials that James had in mind. If James had included sickness among the trials he refers to, then why in chapter 5v14, which was quoted earlier, does he say to those who are sick to call the elders and receive healing, and not tell them to rejoice in their illnesses?

Then there is Paul's thorn in the flesh! How often has this been quoted with little thought or understanding? Firstly, there is no biblical evidence that this 'thorn' was a physical illness. Most commentators over the centuries, including Calvin, believed it was not. It seems much more likely to be those who constantly plagued him with their opposition. The book of Judges refers to the nations that are left in the land being a thorn in the side of the Israelites (see Judges 2:3, also Joshua 23:13).

Secondly, God allowed Satan to bring this thorn into Paul's life because of the incredible level of revelations he had received. When a lady told Smith Wigglesworth that the arthritis she was suffering from was 'her thorn in the flesh,' it is reported that he retorted by asking what exceedingly great revelations of heaven she had received that God saw fit to give her such a thorn. I think some care is needed before claiming anything about thorns in our flesh.

There are three main areas of understanding that we need to come to if we are to give answers to the questions about healing.

Releasing healing on the earth is the church's responsibility

It is God who heals; it is his power and the authority that Jesus has been given that bring healing to sick and infirm bodies, but it is the church's responsibility to release that healing on the earth. We can achieve nothing without his power and anointing, but he requires us to act, to lay hands on the sick, and speak his words of life and healing. When we realise this it changes a whole lot of things. It means we can stop blaming God; stop making excuses and apologising on his behalf; stop blaming people who have not yet been healed as if it is their fault; and very importantly, take our responsibility and seek to learn how to better release the healing power of heaven upon the earth.

One of our problems has been that we have been asking God to do what he has already given us permission to do. We need to take seriously our God given responsibility, and learn to become a church that heals. In addition, we ask God for power that he has already given us, and is waiting for us to start using properly.

Maybe the greatest perplexity in the Christian life is what we perceive as unanswered prayer. We can accept that sometimes the answer is 'no,' but what are we to make of it when there appears to be no answer at all, despite the Bible's promises about asking and receiving, and whatsoever you shall ask for in prayer believe and it will be yours (see Luke 11:9 and Mark 11:24)? I believe God answers prayer because I believe he is true to his Word, but we do not always receive the answer. A while ago, I was travelling home from conducting some training in Argyll in the west of Scotland. I called my wife, Helen, before leaving the town, asking her to call me back in a few minutes. The return call didn't come. I drove a considerable distance through the lovely countryside and passing Loch Lomond before finally receiving Helen's call. Had she ignored me, or been too busy to call back? No, the problem was I didn't have a signal – I wasn't positioned to receive. In 1 Corinthians 2:12 Paul says, "We have not received the spirit of the world but the Spirit who is from God, that we may **understand** what God has freely given us." God is freely giving to us by his grace. We need understanding to receive what he makes available. Here are four keys to help us position ourselves to receive:

1. Humble ourselves, as we depend on and agree with God and his Word.
2. Develop expectant faith based on God's Word.
3. Give praise and thanksgiving in advance.
4. Maintain a generous position of giving and forgiving others. Jesus' promise in Mark 11:24 is followed in verse 25 with an instruction to forgive those who you hold anything against.

In the above steps, we open ourselves up in ways that enable us to receive more fully. This is not a formula that means automatic success, but some key principles that I believe will help us. There are still some major things to consider as we think about why we have not seen more healing.

There are blockages to healing that need to be removed

When healing is released from heaven, it still has to be released on the earth. Here the flow of healing can collide with some barriers that hinder healing in a person's life. These barriers are obstacles that need to be overcome and removed. Isaiah 57:14 says, "Build up, build up, prepare the road! Remove the obstacles out of the way of my people." As we build up a road for healing, in Jesus name, to travel along, we must recognise what this verse says, and remove the obstacles. We cannot remain ignorant of them, or ignore them as if they will just disappear. We need to understand the blockages to God's river of grace from his Word, and learn how to remove them. I wonder how many people have received prayer for healing, felt no difference in their condition and left disappointed, simply because those ministering did not have the wisdom to consider what might be blocking the healing coming to this person. If we do not see immediate change, or no healing takes place, we always ask several questions about what might be the hindrance.

What are the common blockages?

Theological blockages: We have already dealt with this area to a degree. Where people have received teaching that has suggested that God does not heal, or rarely heals, then often a mental blockage is built up that produces doubt, rather than faith. We counter this blockage by teaching the plain truth of the Word of

God. As we soak ourselves in God's Word, so it washes and renews our minds.

Relational blockages: In our experience, this is by far the most common obstacle. Unforgiveness held against those who have wronged us is a huge block to the grace of God operating in our lives. Jesus made it clear, that we must forgive those who have wronged us if we are to benefit from the full extent of God's forgiveness and grace towards us– see Matthew 6:14-15; and 18:21-35. Repeatedly, we have seen people trapped in pain or depression who, as soon as they pronounce their forgiveness to the one who wronged them, are set free and healing begins in their lives, sometimes instantly taking place.

Demonic blockages: Jesus healed people in all sorts of ways – by touch, with a word, at a distance, and also by driving out demons, e.g. in the passage we have referred to before in Mark 9:14-27. A lady in my church had suffered terrible neck pain for some time. Many people prayed with her for healing, but to no avail, and often to her extreme discomfort. As Helen and I ministered to her one day, the Holy Spirit clearly revealed to me that there was a spirit of infirmity afflicting her neck. We cast it off in the name of Jesus, and she was healed instantly! Again, I will discuss more about how demons can affect people in chapter 4, but for now, it is important to recognise that a demonic spirit can in fact cause an ailment or infirmity. Discernment is needed, but where the removal of a demon is required there is little point in just going on praying for healing.

Unconfessed sin: Where there is secret, deliberate sin in a person's life that can, and often will, block God's healing to that individual, though God's mercy is such, that even in such a case healing could take place maybe so that God's kindness might lead to repentance (Romans 2:4). However, it is prudent to make sure you confess and repent of any known sins.

Unbelief: Faith is important in the process of receiving healing. Jesus said to two blind men, '*According to your faith will it be done to you*.' (Matthew 929). Many times he commended people for their faith. Of course such faith in the recipient of healing is not always necessary, hence the many people we see, who do not believe in Jesus, and yet receive healing. Also, we have seen many babies healed; in fact, babies seem much easier to bring healing to than anyone else. Now if a person lacks faith, what do we do? Do we condemn them and make them feel worse? Of course not! Romans 10:17 says, "Consequently, faith comes from hearing the message, and the message is heard through the word of Christ." If someone lacks faith, or is locked in unbelief, then we speak the Word of God to them and share testimonies of healings with them.

Other blockages: These include misunderstanding the ways God brings healing, for example thinking it must always be instant rather than sometimes a process. A sense of hopelessness, particularly where someone may have been given a particularly bad prognosis about his or her condition, can create a mindset that makes it hard to receive anything else. Some people can befriend their illnesses, falling into the pit of self-pity, or embracing the 'benefits' of disability. The question Jesus asked the man at the pool is still relevant at times: 'Do you want to get well?' (John 5:6)

In dealing with these blockages, we are often dealing with the root of the sickness. This is most important, just like pulling weeds by the roots, rather than lazily lopping off their leaves only for them to grow back. This is one of the reasons why we can on occasion find that someone appears to made well, only to become sick again soon after, and often with the same condition.

The benefit of some people praying in agreement and faith over a person for healing is a powerful thing, and almost all people we minister to feel the benefit of that, and sense God's presence and peace strongly upon them. This can lead to symptoms of illness going, and the person feeling that they have been healed. However, if the root has not been dealt with, the symptoms can, and often will, return soon afterwards. If that is the case, do not give up, but go back and get the root dealt with properly.

These are some of the most common personal or individual blockages that we have to help people recognise, dismantle and remove. However, there is still one main area we need to consider in looking at why some are not healed, and why often in the Western church we have seen little healing.

There are corporate blockages

In the Western mindset, we tend to view so much from an individual perspective. Even a number of the Scriptures that refer to 'you' - referring to the church in an area - we have regarded and interpreted individualistically. We have looked at some of the main personal blockages, but that is only part of the story. We are a people, and our lives interplay with each other, and affect each other. I believe there are three main areas of corporate blockages that are hindering healing, and indeed much else from flowing in, and through the church today. These blockages are like dams, clogging up the flow of the river of life, and need to be addressed and removed if we are to see the fulfilment of the vision I spoke of in the first chapter of this book.

One of these, which I shall more fully address in chapter 5, is **the need to give healing away.** For too long churches have focussed healing ministry upon themselves. A key to see more healing in the church is in fact to take healing ministry out of the church. I will come back to this later.

The second corporate blockage is **disunity** in the church. Now we do not all have to agree on everything, and we will not see everything eye to eye, but that is not the point. Unity is about the attitude or spirit of our minds. It is about having a generous attitude towards our Christian brothers and sisters, especially when we do not necessarily agree with them. It is about forgiving again and again. It is about not having to have our way, and considering others before ourselves. It is about refusing to take offence, even when someone gives offence. It is about love covering a multitude of sins. It is about having the humility and grace to admit that you may in fact not be right about everything. True unity is a wonderful, life-giving blessing.

Where disunity has found a place, it will be a great hindrance to the work of God in our midst. The disunity in the Corinthian church was, certainly in part, a cause for sickness and even death among them – it is that serious (see 1 Corinthians 11:30). We do not need to all meet together and worship in the same way or anything like that, but we do need to forgive any wrongs that have taken place, honour one another and maintain an attitude of blessing towards others in our local church and the wider church.

The third area of corporate blockage, probably the most important, and often the most unrecognised, is the area of **unbelief**. Yes, we recognise it at the individual level, but rarely at the corporate level. We find this in two main passages of the New Testament. First as we come to Nazareth in Mark 6:1-6:

Jesus left there and went to his hometown, accompanied by his disciples. When the Sabbath came, he began to teach in the synagogue, and many who heard him were amazed. "Where did this man get these things?" they asked. "What's this wisdom that has been given him, that he even does miracles! Isn't this the carpenter? Isn't this Mary's son and the brother of James, Joseph, Judas and Simon? Aren't his sisters here with us?" And they took offense at him. Jesus said to them, "Only in his hometown, among his relatives and in his own house is a prophet without honor." He could not do any miracles there, except lay his hands on a few sick people and heal them. And he was amazed at their lack of faith.

Jesus was hindered from performing any miracles in his hometown, only being able to heal a few sick people there, due to their lack of faith. This is not referring to particular individuals who lacked faith for their healing, but to the town's lack of faith. This town, partly due to familiarity with Jesus and his family, let their hearts become offended, and sank into unbelief. Even in a place where there are some who believe, the unbelief of the many can be overwhelming. Thankfully, the power of faith is great, and it may actually only take a relatively small number who truly believe to begin tip the balance, starting to overcome the unbelief of the majority.

The second passage takes us back to Mark 9:14-27.
When they came to the other disciples, they saw a large crowd around them and the teachers of the law arguing with them. As soon as all the people saw Jesus, they were overwhelmed with wonder and ran to greet him. "What are you arguing with them about?" he asked. A man in the crowd answered, "Teacher, I brought you my son, who is possessed by a spirit that has robbed him of speech. Whenever it seizes him, it throws him to the ground. He foams at the mouth, gnashes his teeth and becomes rigid. I asked your

disciples to drive out the spirit, but they could not." "O unbelieving generation," Jesus replied, "how long shall I stay with you? How long shall I put up with you? Bring the boy to me." So they brought him. When the spirit saw Jesus, it immediately threw the boy into a convulsion. He fell to the ground and rolled around, foaming at the mouth. Jesus asked the boy's father, "How long has he been like this?" "From childhood," he answered. "It has often thrown him into fire or water to kill him. But if you can do anything, take pity on us and help us." "'If you can'?" said Jesus. "Everything is possible for him who believes." Immediately the boy's father exclaimed, "I do believe; help me overcome my unbelief!" When Jesus saw that a crowd was running to the scene, he rebuked the evil spirit. "You deaf and mute spirit," he said, "I command you, come out of him and never enter him again." The spirit shrieked, convulsed him violently and came out. The boy looked so much like a corpse that many said, "He's dead." But Jesus took him by the hand and lifted him to his feet, and he stood up.

Here we come to a situation, similar to what we might have found ourselves in, where the disciples, who had been left behind when Jesus went up the mountain, were unable to drive out the demon, and heal this boy. Our reaction to being in such a situation must not be to think 'oh well, it didn't work this time,' or 'I guess God didn't want to heal that boy.' Instead, we have to seek earnestly as to why we were powerless, and what can we learn to overcome our inability.

Jesus clearly identifies the problem of unbelief here, and he identifies it on three levels. There is the individual level, which we see in his conversing with the boy's father. The faith or lack of faith of the boy is never in question here. The father has brought the boy, no doubt with a degree of expectancy, having heard of the reputation of Jesus and his disciples to heal the sick and free those oppressed by demons (see Mark 6:7-13 which show us that these disciples already had experience of healing and overcoming demons). However, his expectancy soon turns to disappointment and doubt when the disciples appear unable to help. Therefore, he exclaims to Jesus that he does believe, but needs help to overcome his unbelief.

I imagine many have greatly identified with this man's statement, but unfortunately, I have several times heard Christian people repeat his phrase as if that is OK. You may have been in that position, but you are not to remain there. We have already recognised that unbelief can be an issue and a blockage for the individual, and in this passage, we see how bad experiences can so easily affect faith levels. But here we want to see the corporate area of unbelief. We see this in the other two levels here in this account.

When the disciples are alone with Jesus they inquire of him as to why they were unable to cast out the demon that he dealt with so effectively. In Mark's Gospel Jesus refers to the need of prayer and fasting in verse 29. Many have assumed that there are particular types of evil spirits or illnesses, which require special times of prayer with fasting for us to overcome. While preparation in such a manner is good, and will have benefit, I do not believe that this is the correct understanding of Jesus' words. There are times when we come across sudden need and have to act without time for such preparation. In observing Jesus' life, we do not see him necessarily having special times of fasting before dealing with demons. Most importantly, Jesus gave his disciples authority 'to drive out all demons and cure diseases.' (Luke 9:1) I believe that what Jesus is referring to in verse 29 by 'this kind' is in fact unbelief, and we drive unbelief from our hearts through prayer and fasting. Jesus began his ministry by going into the desert where he fasted and prayed, and came out in the power of the Spirit.

When we look at Matthew's version of this incident, and the disciples ask Jesus the reason why they were unsuccessful, he replies, "because you have so little faith." Therefore, what we find in this passage is that the lack of faith was not just in the heart of the father of the boy, but was also in the band of disciples. Similarly today, we can find churches, or groups of Christians who have so little faith. Where that is the case, it is no wonder that there is little, if any, healing and freeing of oppressed lives taking place among them.

Jesus identifies the final and widest level of unbelief, when he seems to ruefully cry out and identify an unbelieving generation, an unbelieving people. Even if we have great faith, most of us are living in the environment of a people of unbelief, and are often surrounded by scepticism and cynicism. So many lives around us have been coloured by hardships, failures and disappointments, and so produce a rather negative outlook. You might comment to such a person on a beautiful, sunny, cloudless morning about how lovely a day it is. However, they reply, 'Aye, but it'll rain later.'

We are not immune to the spirit of the people we live among, and must recognise that, but also have great hope that our words of faith and our testimonies to the works of God in this day, can and will break through this canopy of unbelief, allowing the flow of heaven's healing power to break loose in our nations.

What has been said in these pages will not answer all the questions that people have about healing, but hopefully it gives some understanding that might help us to move forward, rather than being paralysed by failures and fears. In the midst of seeing many healings, but also in having to deal with times when healing does not come, we need to face this honestly and Biblically, and seek to grow in our understanding and practice. Sometimes we simply have to admit that there can be an element of mystery. Some want it all neatly packaged with easy formulas to follow that bring about results. However, we are dealing with people and we are dealing with the things of God, and it just is not that simple. The revelation we have is that Jesus sends us to proclaim the Good News of the Kingdom and to heal the sick. Real faith can cope with a few mysteries and still believe God. We do not minister healing because it always works, or even sometimes works; we minister healing because Jesus told his disciples to do just that. It really is a matter of obedience.

Chapter 3
Creating a Healing Environment

And the power of the Lord was present for him to heal the sick Luke 5:17

One of our Healing Rooms volunteers came to me one day to say that she had noticed that her problems with asthma had ceased. She was getting work done on her house and there was plenty of dust about, but she had not suffered any adverse reaction. No one had actually prayed with her about this, but she felt just being in the right environment for healing had led to this release. Recently I heard from one of our other rooms that a man, who was in just to observe and see what happened when a friend was being ministered to, found that he had been healed while just sitting in the room without anyone praying for him or ministering to him in any way.

In the last chapter, we recognised that a big part of the blockage to healing is on a corporate level, so it is imperative that we create a corporate environment that is conducive to healing as we seek to be effective healing communities.

The early church clearly witnessed some remarkable healings and miracles. Some of the key features we see in the infant church in the book of Acts are as follows:

1. **EXTRAVAGANT PRAISE:** "They worshipped him and returned to Jerusalem with great joy. And they stayed continually at the temple praising God" (Luke 24:52-53). This was the disciples' response to seeing the Risen Christ.
2. **EXTRAORDINARY PRAYER:** Acts 1:14 says, "They all joined together constantly in prayer." We see the early believers giving themselves to continual prayer for the outpouring of the promised Holy Spirit.
3. **EXCELLENT TEACHING:** "They devoted themselves to the apostles' teaching" (Acts 2:42). The apostles brought teaching that was revelatory and transformed lives, rather than merely informing minds.
4. **EXTREME GENEROSITY:** Acts 2:44-45 tells us, "All the believers were together and had everything in common. Selling their possessions and goods, they gave to anyone as he had need." They were a people of great generosity in their giving.
5. **EXPECTING MIRACLES:** "Everyone was filled with awe, and many wonders and miraculous signs were done by the apostles" (Acts 2:43). Signs, wonders and miracles were an unmistakable feature in the early church.
6. **EXCITING WITNESS:** In Acts 4:20 Peter and John declare, "We cannot help speaking about what we have seen and heard." These believers were giving testimony to the activity of God in and through their lives. Much of their witness and preaching was in explanation of what the people had just seen and heard.

PLOSIVE GROWTH: Acts 2:47 states, "And
Lord added to their number daily those who
were being saved." The above six features of
church life, in co-operation with the Holy Spirit,
resulted in great breakthrough and many
turning to the Lord.

I will comment on a number of these areas throughout
this and other chapters. If we are to experience the
same remarkable fruit and growth, and make a similar
or even greater impact on our present world, then I
believe we need to make these the features of our
church life as well.

The Prerequisite of Intercessory Prayer
When Jesus entered Jerusalem, just prior to his arrest
and crucifixion, he stirred up the whole city and made
the Temple his first stop.

*Jesus entered the temple area and drove out all who
were buying and selling there. He overturned the
tables of the money changers and the benches of
those selling doves. "It is written," he said to them,"*
'My house will be called a house of prayer,' *but you
are making it a 'den of robbers.'" The blind and the
lame came to him at the temple, and he healed them.
But when the chief priests and the teachers of the law
saw the wonderful things he did and the children
shouting in the temple area, "Hosanna to the Son of
David," they were indignant.*
Matthew 21:12-15

He cleared the Temple courts in a forthright manner declaring that this place should be a 'house of prayer.' It is interesting to see the responses to this act. No doubt the sellers of goods and moneychangers were extremely shocked and upset by his actions. The religious rulers were angered and offended while the children sang praises, and the blind and lame, the excluded ones, came and were healed.

Praise and prayer – the first features on the list from Acts – were, and still are, foundational practices for releasing healing. In Ezekiel 47 the river of life, that releases healing flows from the Temple sanctuary, the place of worship and prayer. The healing ministry needs to be saturated in prayer. The practice of all our Healing Rooms is to spend an hour in worship, praising God, listening to him, calling on him and waiting on him before we open our doors. The praise here too was extravagant – the religious people thought it over the top – as the children shouted 'hosanna.' Some today criticize the enthusiasm of others as 'over the top.' But I would ask the question: over the top of what? By whose standard are we measuring this? Those with childlike faith and devotion, who appreciate in ever greater measure what God has done for them, will praise him extravagantly.

Establishing a house of prayer requires extraordinary effort. It means giving priority to and investment in developing a personal and corporate prayer life. This begins in the secret place, for it is those who develop prayer in that place, that will pray powerful and effective prayers in the public place.

What is intercessory prayer and how can it be developed?

There are many types of prayer or ways of praying, and intercessory prayer is one of them (others might be described as personal petition, devotional prayer, Biblical meditation, listening prayer, soaking prayer etc.) Intercession – standing in the gap between the way things are in heaven and the way they are on earth - is more of a lifestyle than just a type of prayer. Intercession may include several of the other types of prayer. We might say intercession is not so much something you do, but what you are and a place you occupy – a place between heaven and earth. When prayers seem to go unanswered, it is more to do with us not fully occupying our place in the process, than it is to do with God ignoring us or refusing us.

Some keys to understand:

(1) Our prayers of intercession are to be motivated by grace, not by guilt. Too often believers have felt they ought to pray more and have been made to feel inadequate in prayer. This causes them to drive themselves out of a wrong motivation or else to give up. No, we must be motivated by the goodness of God and carried along by his grace. It is when we first spend time worshipping and adoring him that we enter that dynamic of prayer moved by grace.

(2) We are to pray as his bride, not as a widow. In the parable of Luke 18:1-8 Jesus is teaching his disciples

to pray without growing faint. In this story, he contrasts God, the good Father, with an uncaring judge. Though that is usually seen clearly, many fail to see that the whole parable is one of contrasts, and that the widow is to be contrasted with us as the bride. How can we be a widow when Jesus is alive? We need to stop praying like the poor, begging widow and start praying with confidence as the bride who moves the heart of God.

(3) If we are to pray effectively and in an above ordinary manner, then we need to learn to pray much in the Spirit.
And pray in the Spirit on all occasions with all kinds of prayers and requests. With this in mind, be alert and always keep on praying for all the saints. (Ephesians 6:18; see also Romans 8:26).

It is vital to pray in and with the Holy Spirit to keep us from praying presumptuous prayers. It is also so beneficial to pray in the Spirit, including praying in tongues, because our flesh so easily weakens and gets so quickly distracted in the place of prayer (at least that is my experience!). When we pray in the Spirit and using the gift of tongues, it is our spirit that is praying. Our body and soul are naturally pulled towards the things of the world, whereas our regenerated spirit is drawn to the things of God's Heavenly Kingdom. If you have never received the gift of tongues simply ask the Father to release this gift in you, believe and then be ready to give it expression (see Luke 11:5-13).

An Outline for Intercessory Prayer
The following outline or model of prayer can be used equally well in a private, personal way as it can in a corporate time of prayer.

1. Beholding the Beauty of the Lord

> *One thing I ask of the LORD, this is what I seek:*
> *that I may dwell in the house of the LORD all the*
> *days of my life,*
> *to gaze upon the beauty of the LORD and to seek*
> *him in his temple.*
> Psalm 27:4

What do we mean by 'beholding his beauty'? His beauty is the combination of his attributes. We need to appreciate and adore the person of Jesus Christ, his character, his names and his activities. The Lord's beauty is never ending and awesome, yet we can fear this intimacy with God. We can easily rush about our lives, and even our worship times, failing to take time to gaze upon him. Why? This seems to be rooted in the fear that comes from our sense of unworthiness and fear of rejection. However, Jesus has dealt with that, and we need to know that we are delighted in by the Lord to free us to delight in Him (see Zephaniah 3:17; Isaiah 62:2-4).

Why is this beholding so important?
Unless we deliberately behold the Lord we will be drawn aside to many other attractions, but as we behold the Lord we are changed more into his likeness (see 2 Corinthians 3:18). As we behold him we cannot but be impressed by him, and he makes his

impression (mark) on us. Therefore, as we come to intercessory prayer, it is vital to take time to behold the wonder and greatness of the Lord to give us a true and effective perspective.

How do we 'behold the beauty of the Lord'?
Make it a priority. Take time. Get set free from any hindering fears. Use the Scriptures, meditating on the names of the Lord. Ask the Holy Spirit to give you revelation of the Lord (Ephesians 1:17) so you might know him more. Then begin to express adoration, love, and devotion to him. Allow this to well up in you and overflow in extravagant praise. Start enjoying the presence of the Lord even if it is only in small measures at first. It will make a difference, and as you pursue his face in this practice, beholding the Lord will become a greater reality in your life.

2. Receiving Revelation
(Revelation 4:1-2; Luke 10:38-42; John 15:15-16).
In Romans 8:26 Paul says, "We do not know what we ought to pray for, but the Spirit himself intercedes for us…" A great obstacle to prayer is our presumption. It is vitally important that we spend significant time listening to the Lord and letting him direct us through spiritual insight and understanding (Colossians 1:9). Paul Bilheimer said, "True prayer begins in the heart of God"

In Revelation 4:1-2 we find an open door, a voice speaking, an invitation − 'come up here' - and a revelation − 'I will show you.' Jesus has opened the way for us to approach the heavenly throne. In that place God is speaking, and like Isaiah we can overhear the conversations of heaven and offer ourselves for his purposes (see Isaiah 6:1-8).

He invites us to come higher, not to settle for where we are, but to enter further into the dimension of revelation, as God wants to show us things so that we will intercede.

In Luke 10:38-42 we have a different picture, not of the throne room of heaven but of a simple room in a home. Here we find Mary who sits at the Lord's feet listening to his word. She refuses to be distracted, like her sister Martha was, for Mary has chosen the better, the one thing that is needed. Similarly, we can sit at Jesus feet, waiting, watching and listening for his word of direction and instruction.

Then in John 15:15-16 we find a picture of friendship. Jesus calls you his friend. We need to develop this friendship and pray out of that relationship. There we find that he has made known to us everything he learned from the Father (see also John 16:12-15). We also discover that we are chosen and appointed to bear fruit, and as we accept and live in that the Father will give us whatever we ask in Jesus name.

In what ways does this revelation come?
It may come in dreams, visions, inner prompts, words, Scriptures, through angels and more. We need to believe and expect revelation. God wants to reveal things to us as he brings us into the process of bringing his will on earth as it is in heaven.

3. Declaring God's Word and Will

To declare means to make known or state clearly (sometimes in the face of contradiction); to announce officially, to proclaim, to state emphatically; to reveal, and to show. 1 Chronicles 16:24 says, "Declare his glory among the nations, his marvellous deeds among all peoples." And Isaiah 42:9 says, "See, the former things have taken place, and new things I declare; before they spring into being I announce them to you."

1 Peter 2:9 states, "But you are a chosen people, a royal priesthood, a holy nation, a people belonging to God, that you may declare the praises of him who called you out of darkness into his wonderful light."

There is power in declaration. As we get hold of God's Word and will (revelation), so we must declare it aloud. As we declare it, faith grows, and as faith grows, we declare even more without doubting. This, of course, must be based on what God says in the *logos* word (Scripture) or by his *rhema* word (prophetic word). We cannot just declare anything and expect fruit from that.

As we declare aloud the words of God, faith is released and the process of fulfillment takes place: faith hears (Romans 10:17); faith sees (Genesis 13:14-15); faith speaks (declares) (Romans 10:10; 2 Corinthians 4:13); faith perseveres (Romans 4:18-21); and faith receives (Mark 11:24). What is loosed in heaven (God declares it) we are to loose on earth as we declare it.

4. Calling Forth the Promises

Romans 4:17 says, "… God who gives life to the dead and calls things that are not as though they were." As we get hold of the revelation God is giving and declare it aloud, then we must press in and call it forth on the earth to see its fruition. (This is where faith perseveres). We are to call forth that which is not (in our earthly reality), as though it were, because it is in God's heavenly reality. We see an example of this with Elijah on Mount Carmel as recorded in1 Kings 18:41-45.

There has been a long drought in the land when Elijah prophesies a heavy rain. However, there is not a cloud in the sky. Elijah has seen in the heavenly realm; he has heard the sound of the rain, and is not deflected off course by what appears to be the situation on the earth. He sends his servant seven times to look for the clouds, while he intercedes calling it forth on earth as it is already in heaven, that is already pronounced by the Lord. Finally, a cloud the size of a man's hand appears in the sky. This is like the first fruits that we see which mean the greater fulfillment is coming along right behind.

How do we 'call things forth'?
1. Believe what God has promised – do not waver, but be fully persuaded (see Romans 4:20-21).
2. Know that the heavenly reality (unseen realm) is greater than the earthly reality (visible realm).
3. Remind God of his promises (he doesn't forget, but it is a Scriptural thing to do).

4. Call these things forth with a determined perseverance.
5. Line your life up with the promises even before you see their fulfillment.

5. Praying the Scriptural prayers
This is a vital practice, praying the divinely inspired words of Scripture means we always know something to pray, and we are agreeing with the Holy Spirit. There are many important prayers in Scripture, for example Psalm 85:4-7; 86:11-13; 144:5, 8; Isaiah 64:1-2 ; Matthew 6:9-13; 9:38; and the prayers of the apostles for the church such as Acts 4:29-30; Romans 15:5-6; 15.13; Ephesians1:17-19; 3:16-19; Philippians 1:9-11; Colossians 1:9-13; 1 Thessalonians 3:11-13; 2 Thessalonians 2:16-17; 3:1-5.

These are all key prayers for the building up and maturing of the church, and we have found Acts 4:29-30 particularly important to use in praying for an outbreak of healing and miracles. I would encourage you to get to know these Scriptural prayers well – learning some by heart and pray them for your church, the church in your community and nation. As you do this regularly do not fear repetition – there is a need to keep asking, and as you do so, you will develop these prayers for your specific situation, finally turning them into worship, thanksgiving and song, knowing that God will answer the prayers of his Word.

6. Bringing people to the feet of Jesus
Matthew 15:30 tells us, "Great crowds came to him, bringing the lame, the blind, the crippled, the mute and

many others, and **laid them at his feet**; and he healed them." In the Gospels we read of people being brought to the feet of Jesus, either in person, or through the request of another, for deliverance (Mark 7:25); for healing (Luke 8:41); and for the raising of the dead (John 11:32).

While it is important to pray with sick people in person when we can, this is not always possible. Sometimes we can only lift them up to Jesus at a distance, or pray with a friend or relation by proxy. We also send prayer cloths that have been anointed with oil and prayed over to those who request them. This has resulted in many testimonies of healing (see Acts 19:12). It is equally important that those we minister to directly for healing are also being lifted up in intercessory prayer.

A young woman of 32 years of age came to our rooms having been diagnosed with tumors on her liver and given only nine months to live. God touched her very powerfully on several occasions in the rooms – she often felt a hand pressing on her body when no one in the team was touching her. Subsequent hospital tests gave her the all clear with no tumors to be found. I am sure a key in all this was that many in her church were continually lifting her up in intercessory prayer.

7. Lifting the arms – covering and lifting up the leaders and workers
In Exodus 17:8-16 we find the Israelites locked in battle against the Amalekites. Essential to how the battle would go was the intercession of Moses on the nearby hillside. As the battle continued Moses grew

tired, so Aaron and Hur held up his arms giving rise to victory in the heavenlies, which led to victory on the earthly battlefield.

The Amalekites were the ones who picked off the weak and weary (Deuteronomy 25:17-18); and later raided and ruined the Israelites crops (Judges 6:3-4). That same spirit is at work today, and it is essential we cover the weak and protect the harvest.

It is also necessary that we pray for workers for God's harvest (Matthew 9:38). We are to ask the Lord to send out (literally thrust or throw out) workers into his harvest field. Having been thrust out, these workers need covered in prayer and have their hands lifted up to keep them strong for the battle. This is needed in many areas of ministry, and very much so in the areas of healing and deliverance, as we take back from the enemy what he has stolen.

Here then is what a session of intercessory prayer could look like.
1. Find a good place. Put away any distractions, give over any concerns to the Lord.
2. Start to praise and worship the Lord. Use good worship music or whatever helps. Behold the beauty of the Lord – focus on an attribute/name of Jesus, e.g. the Good Shepherd. Take plenty of time.
3. Respond to his invitation to come up – the veil is torn, the way is open. Take time to listen to the Lord. Expect revelation – it may come in different ways. Write down what he reveals. If

no revelation comes, that is OK – God is pleased with you taking time just to listen to him.

4. Begin to declare truths about God – who he is, e.g. God Almighty; what he does, e.g. his miracles; what he says and what his will is, e.g. to save people. Declare anything else he is showing you.

5. Call forth what God has promised in his Word and prophetically to you, or for your church, city etc.

6. Take a prayer of Scripture, e.g. Ephesians 1:17-19 and pray it out for your life, your church, and the church in your nation.

7. Bring people you are concerned for to the feet of Jesus, asking him to stretch out his hand of mercy to them. Pray for people you long to see impacted by God. Ask the Holy Spirit to hover over them, bringing forth his light and life to them.

8. Lift up by name church leaders and workers in the harvest field. Pray God's banner over them, and ask him to protect, strengthen and sharpen them in their work.

Recognising the primary place of intercessory prayer in creating and maintaining an environment in which healing can flow, we will now look at some of the other key factors that we have found beneficial.

In our ministry in Scotland, the following five factors are very important to us as we seek to develop the healing ministry and bring in God's Kingdom:

1. Enabling unity of the Body of Christ
2. Equipping the church for harvest
3. Emphasising miraculous expectation
4. Evangelising through healing
5. Exemplifying a good model of healing

I will cover 3 and 4 above in later chapters. In this chapter, I will talk about the other three, along with some other factors for a fruitful environment.

Enabling Unity of the Body of Christ

One of the corporate blockages to healing is of course disunity in the church. Unity is much more than an absence of disunity, just as true peace is much more than an absence of war. A true expression of unity sees God's people working together, flowing together and complementing one another in all their diversity. It is where we can agree together for the purpose of God to come forth, even where we may not see eye to eye on every detail of our faith. It is ultimately where we love each other, prefer each other and look to the interests of other people before our own. We have sought to foster such unity in our teams, and very importantly give a means for the expression of that unity. Unity is not merely sitting around together drinking coffee, no matter how well we get on with each other. Unity must be active and be expressed in action that allows its true power to be demonstrated,

It is as we work together, and work through our diversity, that we truly learn to love one another, honour and respect each other, give encouragement to all, and it is where trust is born and grown. The place of unity is also the place where God's manifest presence seems to show up and remain. The often-quoted 133rd Psalm bears repeating here:

How good and pleasant it is when brothers live
together in unity!
For there the LORD bestows his blessing,
even life forevermore.

The river of life flows in this environment, and the presence of the Lord can become almost tangible.

Equipping the church for harvest
We have trained many hundreds of people on the courses we run with the purpose of equipping them, activating their faith, and releasing them into doing the works of God's Kingdom. There has been enough of people merely being taught, gathering more information, and knowing much but doing little. We do equip by giving teaching from God's Word, but there are other valuable ways of equipping the church.

First, it is important that we realise the purpose for which we are being trained. We need to see the harvest that Jesus had expectation of, and not be stuck in a mentality of just keeping going and holding our head above water. It is time for us to swim – against the tides of this world, but with the flow of the river of life.

Second, we need to be equipped in the Word of God in a way that produces faith. The Word will do that as we hear it, but we need cleansed from all deafness of spirit to hear the revelation Word of God that changes us. We need to hear the Word taught and preached under the quickening of the anointing of the Holy Spirit. That is the excellent teaching referred to earlier. Excellent teaching is that which surpasses the ordinary. It is not about being clever and slick, but about authority and effectiveness that comes through revelation, inspiration and the anointing of the Holy Spirit. This, along with speaking out the testimonies of what God is doing, will lead to an expectant faith. When enough of us together get hold of such expectancy in faith, then the atmosphere can change and anything good can happen!

Third, I see a great need for believers to be equipped and made ready for the task by finding a new level of confidence in Christ. Confidence that he is who he says he is, that he will do what he says he will do, that he is with us, and that he will work through us by his Spirit. We need to be impressed with Jesus, taking time to focus on him, reading regularly of what he did and said in the Gospels, and allowing him to make his impression on us. Only when we gain such confidence in him will we be able to exercise the authority that he has given to us.

Exemplifying a good model of healing
Sadly, there are a good number of people who have been hurt and set back by experiencing healing or deliverance ministry that has been at times unhelpful and unwise, or at other times been conducted in a shoddy or uncaring manner. Frankly, there is no need for this or any excuse. Just because there have been instances of 'bad ministry practice' we do not throw out

all healing and deliverance ministry. Some preachers have no doubt preached some poor and unhelpful sermons, but does that mean we should throw out preaching? Of course not – we should learn to do it more ably. Likewise, as with any other ministry gift, we must always seek to develop a good practice. Jesus went around the country 'doing good and healing all' (Acts 10:38). Moreover, in Mark 7:37 we read that the people said of him; "He has done everything well." Therefore, we want to develop a good practice of healing. We will not get it right every time and it will not be perfect, but we will only grow in this as we do it. If our heart is right towards God and loving towards people, then we can truly develop a good and godly practice.

As we minister to the sick, we are representing Jesus and should be careful to see that we represent him faithfully. Jesus loved people and he healed them. In Luke chapter 9 we read how Jesus sent out his twelve disciples to do what he had been doing. He then gathered them together to get some time alone with them to de-brief. However, the crowds learned where he was and came out to him. This was not convenient, yet v11 says, "He welcomed them and spoke to them about the kingdom of God, and healed those who needed healing."

We are to welcome people in his name and serve them well. There is simply no reason not to treat people well, so that even those who may not immediately receive healing in any way, still feel cared for and testify that it was good that they came to us. It is all about showing Jesus to people, it is never about us looking good or powerful or 'having a ministry.' Jesus dealt with people often very simply. There was not any hype, pretence, exaggeration or manipulation, and there should never be any of this in healing ministry today. When we truly move in the power of God, he does enough through us that there is never a need to add to it our little extras.

What does a good model of healing look like?

In this, we want to do what we see Jesus did and bring in some wisdom that is important for today.

Jesus asked people questions: What do you want me to do for you? How long has he been like this? And so on. We conduct what could be called a short interview, spending a few moments asking the person some introductory questions; e.g. Where does it hurt? How long have you had this condition? How and when did it start? Is there a history of this in your family? Have you had prayer before? If so, what happened?

We can then discern what is really needed as we listen to the person and to the Holy Spirit. Then we have to decide how we are going to pray, depending on whether there is a simple need for physical healing, or a need to deal with forgiveness issues, or maybe a need for deliverance from demonic influence.

We usually ask the person to stand if they are able, as we find people receive better when standing and are less likely to keep engaging in conversation. It is easy with some people to spend ages talking, sometimes unhelpfully, where they focus on all the problems. It is best to get to prayer as soon as possible, as we want each person to have an encounter with the Holy Spirit.

We would ask the person to get into a mode to receive, and explain that it is best for them not to be praying, as it is hard to receive when you are pouring out your heart through prayer. We encourage them to focus on the Lord.

We would also explain to them what we are going to do. This is particularly necessary when ministering to people not used to receiving such prayer. If we are going to lay hands on them, we ask permission and only lay hands on appropriate areas of the body – such as their forehead, shoulders and hands. Always apply a gentle touch and never lean or push! If the area is a sensitive area like the abdomen or hip, we may ask the person receiving prayer to put their hand on the affected area and then place our hand on their hand. We always seek to have women lay hands on women and men on men in such cases. It is also good practice always to have a woman present when praying with a woman and a man present when praying with a man. It just makes sense, yet I have seen in numerous places people failing to observe this wisdom sometimes leading to real trouble.

As we minister healing, our words and prayers should line up with the Word of God and bring forth edification, exhortation and comfort. It is good to speak out words of affirmation and assurance of God's immense love for this individual.

We always pray with our eyes open to be better aware of what the Holy Spirit is doing and to watch the expression of the person. We can also watch other team members to see when and if they have something to add or pray. If needed, quote Scripture on healing to build faith – never ever rebuke their perceived lack of faith. We will address, if appropriate, any 'blockages' in their life.

If any form of demonic manifestation occurs, we should deal with it decisively if appropriate, e.g. casting off a spirit of infirmity, or bind and move on if it appears to be something more complex. In speaking to the person afterwards, we would want to advise them to make a private appointment to take things further.

At the end of the prayer session – that is when the person is healed or we sense that we have done all that God wants us to do for now - ask the person what they felt. Never be afraid to ask. Then give them some follow-up advice. Invite them to return for more prayer if they have to. We always let them know that we are committed to pray for them until they are healed. Encourage them to give thanks to the Lord.

We never give medical advice and never tell people to throw away their medication. If they appear to be healed then they should go back to their doctor. The person who prescribes the medication should be the one they consult about coming off it.

Perseverance is most important in this ministry as it is in all ministries in God's Kingdom. When we start, we must be prepared to finish. Matters can appear to get worse before they get better. When the Israelites cried out to God, and Moses came and confronted Pharaoh, deliverance from their plight did not happen straight away. In fact, things got worse. The slaves were now ordered to collect their own straw and make the same quota of bricks as before when the straw was supplied for them. This caused the people to cry out against Moses. When we pray for the sick, occasionally some can appear to get worse at first, maybe as blocks to healing are confronted. It is vital we do not stop short or lose heart, but persevere through all the way.

If we are prepared to develop and persevere with good models of healing, then we will overcome the problems that have been related to healing ministry in the past. If we work with people through the process of healing and are willing to persevere with them, then we can overcome the difficulty of disappointment. Not only that, but we will see many people healed as God graciously stretches out his hand through us.

I finish this chapter with a testimony to good practice from one of our rooms.

"I went for prayer for osteoarthritis. I just stopped to ask about Healing Rooms and if I could go in. I had an open mind and heart. I was amazed at the love and care they showed to me. Anyway, they laid hands on me and prayed for God to heal my arthritis; I had had a lot of pain in all my joints for about 15 years. That was on Monday, the next morning I woke and I had no pain

in my joints at all. For a whole week I kept thinking about my healing and thought if God could do that for me, then I wanted more. So I returned and asked for prayer for God to heal my depression (clinical) and for God to prosper me in my business. After they prayed for me this morning I felt different inside. I hope that whoever reads this will turn again to God that he may heal you too."

Chapter 4
Going Deeper:
Healing Damaged Lives

Can plunder be taken from warriors,
or captives rescued from the fierce? Isaiah 49:24

In the late 1980's we began to follow the command of Jesus to heal the sick. As we prayed for people for healing and saw the anointing of the Holy Spirit fall upon them, we soon discovered that his presence caused deeper things to rise to the surface. Helen and I soon found ourselves having to learn quickly how to start dealing with demonic strongholds and minister what was commonly called inner healing. Likewise, as we minister to many people in the Healing Rooms, we find that a good number of them require something more; they need healing that reaches into the depth of their beings.

There are too many people, both in the church and outside of the church, living their lives subject to all manner of fears, inner pain and torment. Many of these people feel as if they are in the grip of an enemy too powerful for them to overcome. So can these captives be rescued?

He reached down from on high and took hold of me;
he drew me out of deep waters.
He rescued me from my powerful enemy,
from my foes, who were too strong for me.

They confronted me in the day of my disaster,
but the LORD was my support.
He brought me out into a spacious place;
He rescued me because he delighted in me.
Psalm 18:16-19

David in writing this Psalm was reflecting on the
struggles and pains he experienced in his life. He
celebrates the delivering power of the Lord, who lifted
him out of deep waters and rescued him from enemies
from whom he could not save himself. The Lord brings
him into a place where his life can prosper and
flourish. The Lord does all this for him because he
delights in him. Similarly, the Lord delights in us, and is
most willing and able to draw us out of the depths of
darkness, depression or despair. Recognising that
there are forces in this life that are too strong for us -
primarily the power of sin - is the first step. As we then
turn to the Lord (repent) and co-operate with him, he
will set us free and place our feet upon a rock.

I not only believe from what Scripture says that God
can do this, I have witnessed it on many occasions.
Over the years in our ministry, we have seen the
power of depression break off, the power of drug
addiction shattered, and lives that have been
horrendously abused being restored and made new.

Deeper Healing
We are to declare the full Good News of Jesus Christ
so that those who believe in him might come to know
true **forgiveness, freedom** and **fullness** of life.

Jesus has completed his work. On the cross, he cries out, "It is finished!" (that is complete, made perfect). However, we have to fully lay hold of, apprehend, and then apply what he has accomplished. The truth is that many believers in Jesus do not walk in freedom and do not live the life they could be living. The need is to bring the Body of Christ into the fullness and mature person that God has called us to be, equipped in every way to do the works of his Kingdom (see Ephesians 4:11-13.)

For this to happen we must enter into the truth of what Christ has done for us:
For he has rescued us from the dominion of darkness and brought us into the kingdom of the Son he loves, in whom we have redemption, the forgiveness of sins! (Colossians 1:13 – 14)

We need therefore to come out from believing lies and half-truths, so that we can grow into maturity. We need to come into a true knowledge of God and of who we are in relation to him. Our identity must come from who God says we are and what he says about us. Our key prayers are therefore what Paul prayed two thousand years ago, and these are still as important and relevant today:

I keep asking that the God of our Lord Jesus Christ, the glorious Father, may give you the Spirit of wisdom and revelation, so that you may know him better. I pray also that the eyes of your heart may be enlightened in order that you may know the hope to which he has called you, the riches of his glorious inheritance in the saints, and his incomparably great power for us who believe. (Ephesians 1:17-19)

I pray that out of his glorious riches he may strengthen you with power through his Spirit in your inner being, so that Christ may dwell in your hearts through faith. And I pray that you, being rooted and established in love, may have power, together with all the saints, to grasp how wide and long and high and deep is the love of Christ, and to know this love that surpasses knowledge—that you may be filled to the measure of all the fullness of God. Now to him who is able to do immeasurably more than all we ask or imagine, according to his power that is at work within us, to him be glory in the church and in Christ Jesus throughout all generations, for ever and ever! Amen. (Ephesians 3:16-21)

We then also must take our responsibility to walk in the truth and to resist the lies and works of the devil:

Submit yourselves, then, to God. Resist the devil, and he will flee from you. Come near to God and he will come near to you. Wash your hands, you sinners, and purify your hearts, you double-minded. (James 4:7-8)

As we minister in this area of deeper healing, our aim is not merely to bring relief from pain and problems but to bring about transformation of lives. God does not fix up the old; he brings us into being a new creation. We must not minister to the old man, to self- esteem or self anything else, but call forth the new man in Christ. It is a work of healing, but more than that, it is a work of discipling and equipping people to live in greater fullness of life, not controlled by past wounds but instead led by the Spirit of God. It is setting people free to act rather than always reacting out of woundedness. This is a work of bringing people out from being a victim, and into a victorious walk in the grace and power of Christ.

As we actively engage in deeper healing, we have found the following to be keys for this work:

1. We depend on and expect the leading of the Holy Spirit. We very much rely on the Spirit's leading and have great expectancy of him doing just that. He wants to free and heal people more than we do, and we discover him working in amazing ways as he clearly leads people through some deep memories and areas of their life, and into a place where they can flourish.
2. We work with those who want God's transforming of their lives. This is not for those who want to wallow in their problems, or talk endlessly about how hurt they have been. This is for those who want to be truly changed and who want what God desires for them, and who want to come out of the traps and into a fruitful life.
3. Forgiveness is absolutely foundational.
4. Agreeing with God's truth and coming out of agreement with lies that have been believed is the other major foundation of this ministry.
5. Those receiving ministry have to be willing and ready to take responsibility for their lives.

6. Revelation into the root causes is not only necessary to bring lasting freedom, but also means that what might have taken months to discover through other means can be brought to the light in minutes.
7. Releasing the person further into their God appointed destiny always has to be the final outcome.

The following eight areas of ministry are the key steps in the process of bringing deeper healing to individuals.

1. Receiving forgiveness and forgiving others
The starting point is always in the area of forgiveness of sin, because ultimately it is sin that destroys life. Confessing any known sin; receiving God's forgiveness; forgiving yourself and accepting yourself as forgiven, are vital at the outset of any healing and transforming work. Choosing to forgive those who have wronged you, or who you perceive to have wronged you, is an equally important step (see Ephesians 1:7; 1 John 1:9; Matthew 6:12 & 14-15; Colossians 3:13).

The reason people come for prayer ministry will often be to do with hurt, pain, fear or a sense of oppression. While we would begin there, in order to make any real progress we must make sure the area of forgiveness is properly covered. Forgiveness is foundational, and as we have all sinned and been sinned against forgiveness is essential to living a life of freedom. F. B Meyer said, "Forgiveness is the exclusive prerogative of Christianity." Only God can forgive our sins, and we as representatives of Jesus Christ pronounce the truth of his forgiveness to the one who truly confesses and repents.

The greatest problem of the human heart is pride as it keeps us from God. It is the refusal to accept grace as grace. Even when a person has been greatly damaged in life, there can still be a stronghold of pride in their heart. This is the primary sin we must confess so we can find God's help and healing.

Another great power that damages life is shame. In the Garden, Adam and Eve sinned by eating of the forbidden fruit in an attempt to be independent of God. This of course led to an awareness of their nakedness resulting in a sense of shame. Shame comes from what we have done and what has been done to us, and goes inwards destroying as it goes. Forgiveness slays shame. Knowing you are forgiven and truly forgiving those who have wronged you disables the destructive power of shame.

All sin needs forgiven, but we recognise that there are particular areas of sin that can commonly lead to doors in our lives being opened to oppressive forces. These could be classified in the following areas: sexual sin; occult involvement; hatred and unforgiveness; fear especially the fear of rejection; and generational sins (that is sins and sinful patterns that have been in the family line and seem to be passed on in some ways from one generation to the next).

In a healing session, it is often helpful for the person who is receiving ministry to confess aloud any known sins, especially in these areas. Those ministering can then on the basis of God's Word pronounce God's forgiveness to the person. Many find it hugely beneficial to hear that expressed audibly to them (see 1 John1:9 and James 5:16).

When it comes to forgiving others there are some important things of which we need to be aware. Firstly, it is not so much what is done to us that will affect and harm us but how we respond to what has been done to us.

Secondly, we must recognise that forgiving others is always a choice we can make. Jesus never commands us to do what we cannot do in his grace. We have worked with a number of people who have been terribly abused and there was no way they felt like forgiving their abusers. However, when they came to the recognition that this was what God requires, and through this they themselves will be freed, they made a decision with their will to release those who had sinned against them. Invariably this act of the will opened the floodgates for God's healing grace to pour in and in time heal the emotional torment.

Thirdly, we discover that releasing others frees us but refusing to forgive others allows them and the wrongs they have committed against us to continue to trespass in our lives. We are not letting them totally off the hook – they are still answerable to God but as we forgive, we remove the trespassing and cancel the debt. They now owe us nothing so there are now no obligations and no ties between them and us. On private property, we sometimes see signs stating that trespassers will be prosecuted. We need to develop hearts that hold up a sign saying 'trespassers will be forgiven.'

2. Renouncing lies and breaking wrong agreements

God wants to release us from the powerful effect of lies and deception. These are especially damaging when they have effected our core beliefs about God, our lives and ourselves. In John 8:32 Jesus says, "And you shall know the truth and the truth shall make you free." We need to identify and renounce any lies we have believed about God, ourselves, and about life. We need to break any wrong and false agreements we have made that are against the truth of God's Word.

Sin empowers the enemy but forgiveness undoes his holds (see 1 John 3:5 and 3:8). Lies can keep us trapped even where God has forgiven us. The truth only sets us free when we know it and believe it.

There are a number of types of wrong agreements that we can enter into throughout our lives that we need to identify, repent of and break (this must be done by the spoken word):

Wrong vows e.g., 'I will never trust again.'
Judgments of others e.g. 'it was all his fault.'
Bitter root judgments e.g., 'I will never be like my father/mother.'

Ungodly soul-ties e.g. with a sexual partner outside of marriage; or an abusive or manipulative relationship. We have soul-ties with those people we are in close relationship or connection with. These can be good and healthy, such as in marriage. They can also be ungodly, such as through sexual abuse or control and manipulation.

Ungodly covenants e.g. oaths taken in Freemasonry.

Curses or words of power that have been spoken over you e.g. 'you'll always fail.' In this case, where words have been spoken over us, it is important for us to forgive the one who spoke them.

We then need to come into agreement with the truth of God's Word. When we confess sin, we come into agreement with God's verdict on sin. When we confess the truth of God's Word about our lives we come into agreement with God's verdict about us as his children, bought and cleansed by the blood of Jesus. We come into agreement with the affirmation of the Father, not the accusation of the evil one.

The lies we might have believed throughout our lives, which have often been reinforced by difficult circumstances or by being rejected and put down, can create strongholds in our minds and build in patterns of faulty thinking. These patterns may need some time to be dismantled properly and for new patterns of true, godly thinking to be established. Taking time to reinforce the truth of God's Word into our minds is a most valuable practice, which gives the Holy Spirit the ammunition he needs to renew our minds.

3. Removing layers of fear, hurt, trauma, and hatred.

There are experiences in our lives, which have a fundamental impact upon us. The impact can be long lasting because of the ways in which we interpret these events, the lies we subsequently believe and our sense about God's involvement or non-involvement. If there are several such experiences then they can build layers of wounding, and as a result, we can erect layers of defences. We need to allow the Holy Spirit to bring revelation to the roots of these experiences that there might be a fundamental shift in our inner being. While the actual experiences may have been very wrong, the continuing and devastating effects do not need to rule us any longer.

Key steps to bring healing:
1. Choose to forgive those who have wronged us.
2. Ask the Lord to reveal in his light how this experience affected us: How did this event impact us? Did we believe any lies? Have we responded sinfully to this?
3. Repent of sinful responses and renounce lies.
4. Invite the healing presence of Jesus into these areas. Let him minister by His Spirit.
5. Remove the layers:

Displace fear with the love of God (1 John 4:18).

Apply the balm of Jesus presence to areas of hurt.

Where there has been a traumatic affect this can cause a fracturing – here we pray and call the person together in Christ.

Release through confession and forgiveness from any hatred and self-hatred.

In this ministry the prayer of Ephesians 3:16-19 is very important:

*I pray that out of his glorious riches he may **strengthen you with power through his Spirit in your inner being**, so that Christ may dwell in your hearts through faith. And I pray that you, **being rooted and established in love**, may have power, together with all the saints, to grasp how wide and long and high and deep is the love of Christ, and to know this love that surpasses knowledge—that you may be filled to the measure of all the fullness of God.*

Major times of wounding in our lives can cause a breaking up of our inner being; hence, people say they are 'falling apart'. Christ comes to bring wholeness - he wants to integrate us, drawing us together under him.

4. Releasing from demonic interference
Once we have confessed sin, forgiven others, broken wrong agreements and removed the layers of wounding, then we have taken away the 'legal ground' that any demonic interference/oppression might have had. We can now displace any demonic deposits and activities with that which is true and good in Christ. We do not search for demons, but will at times come across demonic activity in the healing process.

The question that is sometimes raised here concerns how a Christian can be affected by a demon. Notice the use of the terms demonic interference or demonic oppression, which I have been using. Unfortunately, most of our Bible translations use the term 'demon possessed', which of course is a severe and even frightening term. It is unfortunate that they use this term, because essentially it is an inaccurate translation of the Greek word. The wide acceptance of this term in the Western church may be partly due to the lack of experience in dealing with the demonic. Having dealt with many such cases I have never come across anyone who I would term 'possessed.' Sometimes, at the moment of casting out a demon, the oppressed person may appear momentarily out of control with occasional disturbing manifestations as happened in Jesus ministry (see e.g. Mark 9:26).This does not mean that their general life is like that. Many people who need deliverance ministry are affected only in very subtle and often unseen ways, but maybe living with inner torment.

When someone comes to Christ, he or she becomes a new creation in him, but still needs to appropriate and apply what Christ has won for them. It is like a house that someone buys. If you buy a house it is yours, you have the title deeds, and it is now under new ownership. If you discover squatters in the house, you have to evict them. If you discover dry rot in the house, you have to get it removed. The presence of the squatters or the dry rot does not in any way deny or affect your ownership of the house. As a Christian, you are bought and redeemed by the blood of Jesus, but there may be some things that need evicting. To deny this is to condemn those who are oppressed to having to live with that misery, but wisely recognising the need to deal with demonic spirits opens the way for those people to find true freedom.

The devil is a legalist and a liar. He gains ground in people's lives through the avenues of sin. When sin is forgiven his ground is taken away, but being a liar, he tries to bluff those who have been oppressed into believing he still has the right to be there. If someone is trespassing in a private club, they may stay there until someone confronts them and has them put out. When we work through points 1 -3 above in a thorough manner, then the actual act of evicting demonic intruders is quite straightforward. Jesus has given us power to heal the sick and authority to drive out demons.

Here are the key steps for removing and displacing demonic interference:
1. Bind any spirits from interfering in the process.
2. Renounce specifically any spirit that is identified.
3. Cast out/off in the name of Jesus Christ.
4. Pray for filling of the Holy Spirit, and in particular for him to bring the opposite of the spirit that has been cast away.
5. Draw near to God and resist the devil.

Some demonic interference is slight and is easily dealt with, but on occasions we come across severe oppression which can be well entrenched into the personality. In such cases, it is wise to involve experienced people and be well covered in prayer. We should not fear the demonic, but seek to follow Jesus' example in setting the captives free.

These first four stages have examined how we bring people out of darkness. The next four stages outline some principles for bringing people into the fuller life of the Kingdom of God. It is not enough only to set a person free from that which has held them; we must help them move into a positive life for God, otherwise they may slip back into the old ways.

5. Realising our new identity in Christ.
As we walk in agreement with God's Word, we must accept and agree with our new identity of who we are in Christ. There is a need to agree continually with God's affirmation of who we are as his children, so we can walk in the security of his love and grow into the significance of a fruitful life. A sense of personal security and significance is vital to our well-being. We need to let the Father define who we are and what we can achieve. This is not just to make us feel good about ourselves – believing 'good' lies can have that effect. It is to release us to be fruitful and to fulfill God's purpose for our lives.

We need therefore to realise fully this new identity. The word 'realise' has two important meanings for us here: first to become conscious of or aware of something, and second to bring to fruition. If someone sends you a cheque in an envelope you realise (become conscious of) this when you open the envelope. Until then you may have no idea what the envelope contains. However, you do not fully realise (bring to fruition) the value of that cheque, until you cash it or pay it into your bank account. A cheque sitting on your kitchen table or study desk will not buy you anything.

Likewise, we need not only to become conscious of what the Word of God says about our identity in Christ, but we need to start living in the truth of it to realise its full value.

For example, God's Word declares that he has made those who are in Christ righteous. However, some Christians still refer to themselves as 'sinners' saved by grace. Sounds spiritual, but if you still define yourself as a sinner you are likely to keep on sinning. Now some have grasped the truth that he has made them righteous and might refer to themselves in such a manner. However, if they continue to live under an assumption that they are *bound* to sin they have not fully realised this truth of their identity. The need is to go further and actually live out of this truth producing the fruit of righteousness. (This is of course Christ's righteousness bestowed on us and not self-righteousness).

There are many great Bible verses that describe our new identity, and these are well worth meditating on and declaring aloud until they are established in us. (See John 1:12; John 15:5, 15-16; 1 Corinthians 3:16; 12:27; Philippians 3:20 and many more).

6. Relating to God
Once we find freedom from what bound and influenced us negatively, it is vital that we move forward into a

deeper relationship with God as Father. To do this we need to live out of the Spirit of Wisdom and Revelation:

*I keep asking that the God of our Lord Jesus Christ, the glorious Father, **may give you the Spirit of wisdom and revelation, so that you may know him better.** I pray also that the eyes of your heart may be enlightened in order that you may know the hope to which he has called you, the riches of his glorious inheritance in the saints, and his incomparably great power for us who believe.*
(Ephesians 1:17-19)

We need to learn to hear from him, rather than listen to the other voices we may have given our attention to in the past, such as voices of accusation and condemnation. As we meditate on Scripture and spend time listening to the Lord, we will develop a closer relationship with Jesus. Crucial to all this is the need to receive the fullness of the Holy Spirit, learning to walk with and keep in step with the Spirit (Galatians 5:16-25). Any relationship needs time spent on it and a certain amount of work invested into it. It is no different in our relationship with God – Father, Son and Holy Spirit.

7. Responsibility for our walk with God
As we come into greater freedom, it is our responsibility to guard and keep what God has worked in us. There is an unfortunate tendency in some places to expect to receive prayer from others and that this will make everything well. This attitude also shows up

in the inclination to blame God, or the church, or circumstances when things wrong. This overly passive approach is not Biblical and will lead to a person regressing in time. We need to take responsibility for our actions and we need to be deliberate in seeking to grow in God's grace (see Philippians 3:12-14). One way we can do this is by building a hidden life of godly discipline. We need to establish a practice of daily worship, prayer and Bible reading. It is good to develop this in the secret place as taught by Jesus in Matthew 6:1-18. Practicing generosity alongside prayer and fasting makes a mighty combination.

Being deliberate in making decisions to grow in areas of discipleship is necessary. We need to give attention to areas of our lives that we require to grow in, making them a point of focused prayer and effort.

Finally, we must resist the devil in all areas. No more excuses of 'the devil is giving me a hard time' – we need to start giving him a hard time! It is our responsibility to resist as we draw near to God (James 4:7-8). As Paul says in Romans 13:14, "Put on the Lord Jesus Christ, and make no provision for the flesh."

8. Releasing into ministry
Finally, we enter more into our calling, taking hold of the ministry into which the Lord is leading us. It is time to receive training and anointing, and begin to reach out in the power of the Holy Spirit in partnership with other believers. Ask yourself what you desire to do? What makes you come alive? Then go out and start

seeking to live in that way under the guidance of God and godly people.

The Power of Blessing

The LORD bless you and keep you;
the LORD make his face shine upon you and be
gracious to you;
the LORD turn his face toward you and give you
peace.
So they will put my name on the Israelites, and I will
bless them.
Numbers 6:24-27

In the deeper healing process, we work through these areas with people seeking to take them into a place of growing in maturity and freedom, and being able to give to others.

There is another element in the process that we find enormously meaningful and liberating, and that is the power of blessing.

To bless means to affirm, to nurture, to bring to life, and to want and to speak good towards someone. It is the opposite of to curse. Cursing seeks to hinder and destroy life, whereas blessing seeks to expand life and cause it to flourish. Blessing calls people into their full potential. There is great power in words as Proverbs 18:21 makes abundantly clear: "The tongue has the power of life and death, and those who love it will eat its fruit."

The blessing of a person shows acceptance of them, affirms who they are, nurtures and calls forth their stature and potential, and grants permission to them to be all they can be, and to do what they are called and gifted to do. In the act of blessing, we will prophesy a special future for the person in Christ.

Everyone needs blessing, but it has proved particularly useful and fruitful to impart a father's and/or mother's blessing to those who in some ways have been deprived of that in their early years of life. A father is especially important in the affirming of his children and mothers have a vital role particularly in the nurturing area, though in some ways each of them performs both affirming and nurturing.

How do we give the blessing?
1. We ask their permission and if they want to receive a blessing.
2. We explain that a blessing is a spiritual impartation, and must be received in their spirit and not analysed with their mind.
3. We embrace the person in an appropriate manner and speak the blessing into their body, soul and spirit, sealing the words in the name of Jesus.

Here is an example of the sort of prayer I would use blessing someone (in this case a man we will call John). I would be giving him a father's blessing, not as his father but as a father representing the Fatherhood of God. The wording will of course vary as we are aware of the person's needs and as the Holy Spirit leads us.

Father God, I thank you for John and that you love him with an eternal love. I bless you John today as a father, and thank God that he knitted you together in your mother's womb. I declare that it was very good that you were born, and that you are loved and wanted, and that you bring pleasure to others.

I call you forth through all you have experienced in life to grow and come to be the mature man that God intends you to be. I declare that you are very good and able to do all things through Christ who strengthens you. I affirm you as a man of God, and give you permission to try, to do all things well, and to reach your potential in life.

I release you to do mighty things for God in your life, to be a loving father and faithful husband. I now seal this blessing in the name of Jesus. Amen

There are two final areas I want to speak about in this chapter. These are particular ways in which I have experienced the Lord lead me in ministering to some of the most broken lives.

Healing Fragmented Lives
Fragmented means broken which is a translation of the Hebrew 'shabar' (see Isaiah 61:1 also Psalm 34:18; 147:3). We are to 'bind up the brokenhearted'. To bind means to bandage, tie, pull together, and also to govern. Scripture speaks of two types of breaking in a person:

1. That which the Lord does to remove pride, impurity, independence etc. (see Psalm 51:8, 17).
2. Breaking which the enemy and sinful actions do which destroy life.

Here we are concerned with bringing healing to the second of these. (When God is doing the breaking then we keep well out of the way).

Proverbs speaks of broken or crushed spirits:
15:4 *The tongue that brings healing is a tree of life, but a **deceitful tongue crushes the spirit**.*
15:13 *A happy heart makes the face cheerful, but **heartache crushes the spirit***
17:22 *A cheerful heart is good medicine, but **a crushed spirit dries up the bones**.*
18:14 *A man's spirit sustains him in sickness, but **a crushed spirit who can bear?***

What do we notice from these texts?
Heartache (broken heartedness) crushes the spirit of a person. A crushed spirit dries up, or withers the very bones and is unbearable. If a person has a crushed spirit, they will keep on struggling and getting sick. Sometimes people's spirits shut off, and we call this a 'slumbering spirit' which needs awakened.

When a person is severely torn apart, broken or crushed it will lead to mental health problems - a kind of 'schizo' condition. When I sought the Lord about healing for such conditions, he revealed to me that in some people there has been 'a pulling apart of their mainframe'. A mainframe is a large computer at the hub of a system or a central processing unit (like our brain). He showed me that two of the forces that often pull this apart are rebellion and rejection (these may have been in the family line). Rebellion (active) and rejection (passive) are two very common responses to wounding or damaging factors in a person's life.

So how do we heal and restore all this?
Psalm 86:11 says, "Teach me your way, O LORD, and I will walk in your truth; give me an **undivided heart**, that I may fear your name."

First, we want to bring healing to any brokenness of heart, binding the heart in Christ. (True fear for his name removes the power of all other fear). Then we deal with any rebellion and/or rejection roots going through the process of forgiving, agreements etc. Then we bring restoration to the crushed spirit, breathing in the fresh life of the Holy Spirit through prayer. Finally, we bring everything together under **one Head, Christ** - that is, integrating the person in Jesus. See Ephesians 1:10 and Colossians 1:17.

We are bringing a fundamental shift into the person's inner being so that they can start processing life's events, and relating to life, in a new way.
We are bringing full restoration through:
1. Foundation of Christ's love – Ephesians 3:16-19; compare where people have no stability.
2. Focus of the Holy Spirit (God's will) – John 16:12-15; compare people who are 'all over the place.'

3. Functioning in Kingdom lifestyle – Matthew 6:33; compare those who 'can't get anything done.'

Healing Crooked Roots

What do we mean by a 'crooked root'? The Lord showed me that some people, who despite lots of prayer and taking the right steps still seem to struggle, have in fact a crooked root at the foundation of their life. This leads to everything being built on a foundation that is slightly askew, so that even when they build good practices into their life things still seem a bit off line.

How can this be corrected and healed?

1. We go back to the foundation of the person's life bringing healing and/or deliverance to the very root of their being (asking the Spirit for wisdom and revelation)
2. As they are now a new creation, we declare that over them, and place Jesus as the cornerstone of their life and very being. We call everything to now line up with Christ the cornerstone (See Ephesians 2:20; Isaiah 28:16; 1 Peter 2:6), so they will no longer be disturbed, dishonoured, disgraced or shamed.
3. The outworking of this new alignment needs to be in a place of true fellowship, so *together with all the saints* (Ephesians 3:18) they will know Christ's love, and be rooted and established in this (See also Eph. 2:19-22; 3:16-19).

Bringing the healing of Jesus Christ to damaged lives is one of the most rewarding areas of Christian ministry. It is wonderful indeed to see someone set free, who has been kept captive to fear, bound up by the wounds of abuse, troubled by constant confusion, or tormented by inner conflicts. It is truly glorious to see the burdens of the years fall off, a smile come across their face, and their true personality come to life. There are many people in need of this deeper healing. They need a church to rise up that can minister to them out of the depth of the love of Christ.

Chapter 5
Healing as a Sign and a Wonder

Stretch out your hand to heal and perform miraculous signs and wonders through the name of your holy servant Jesus Acts 4:30

One evening as I was sitting quietly praying and reflecting on the Word of God, I sensed the Holy Spirit whisper in my ear a clear and forceful command: *you are to loose healing as a sign of the Kingdom.* I have sought to follow that instruction for some years now, believing it is both a Biblical decree and a necessary injunction for today. In order to loose healing in this outward way, we need to release this ministry from the confines of church services and church buildings, and release it as a sign and a wonder. We still hold occasional healing services in church buildings, but have recognised that the primary purpose of healing in the New Testament was as a sign and wonder to those outside the believing community. Our emphasis and practice must reflect this, and if it does, we will undoubtedly see much more fruit. This has been our experience over many years now.

As I said earlier in the book, we used to see in our church's ministry many more people from outside of the church being healed than those in the church. When our teams went out on the streets of Glasgow late at night, taking food and hot drinks to those in need, we witnessed numerous miraculous healings.

We would see swollen body parts shrink back to normal as members of the team laid hands on people in Jesus name. One girl, due to have her leg amputated after years of injecting drugs, was miraculously healed, and when she went to the hospital the next day was sent away with a clean bill of health. We met her some time later and discovered she was now working as a drugs counselor, and put the change in her life down to the night two ladies laid hands on her for healing on a dark Glasgow street.

In our current ministry, we are seeking to make the healing ministry of Jesus accessible and available to all the people of our nation. It is great when sick and desperate people are on their way to the shops, only to come across the place of prayer, and find healing and salvation. We have a Healing Room in an awesome location in the town of Greenock right in the main shopping centre. One woman wrote this testimony:

"When I passed a crowd of people in the mall I thought, 'what's going on' and then I saw the words 'prayer and healing room', and I thought I need that! I was so down and depressed for such a long time I really wanted to kill myself. I thought no-one could help me, yet I wanted help so much. So I went in for prayer and felt a burning feeling on my head but no hands were on my head. Within three days the depression had gone and I knew I was well."

And here's another one from our rooms in Edinburgh, which operate in a community flat:

"About 4 years ago I suffered a severe mental breakdown and was on anti-depressants. During this time I became involved in drugs and drink, which drove me to things I never imagined I would be involved in. I was on sleeping pills and pills for anxiety from the doctor. I was also suffering from severe paranoia. By doing what I had done for the past 4 years I felt like I had destroyed my life. I was trying to come back, yet the after effects were torture. I was thinking about giving up. I was also filled with a great deal of negative energy. I had a bad spirit with me as my companion, willing me to go back down to where I just came from.

I was going to, until one day, I was walking to the shops and saw the sign for Healing Rooms. I know Jesus led me in there. I asked for prayer explaining my circumstances. That day I received the Holy Spirit and experienced God's presence in a real and amazing way. I realised that I didn't need short term substances to block my pain and wake up feeling terrible about it. I had the real thing.

Since I have had the power of prayer my paranoia, anxiety and insomnia have all gone. So is the negative energy, which I now know was a demon. I have since become a born again Christian and am a totally different person. I don't recognise myself, but I love it. I am continuing to walk God's path and he has healed me emotionally and mentally. As for drink and drugs, well I just pray to Jesus and he gives me what I need, his love."

I love these stories. They illustrate what Jesus can do, when we make him available and release his healing as a sign of the Kingdom. The Kingdom is of course his rule and reign; healing demonstrates his rule over sickness and through this introduces people to the King.

In chapter 3 I referred to seven features of the early church. In this chapter, we shall see how three of them come together: expecting miracles, exciting witness and explosive growth. In the previous chapters, we have been thinking about why we have not seen more healings and what we can do about this. We have discussed the need to address personal and corporate blockages to healing, and the need of a good healing environment, a true community of faith. Now we see that another key to seeing more healing is to give this ministry its true focus – reaching lost people. I believe that as we give it away, we, in fact, will receive more healing in the church body.

Expecting Miracles, Signs and Wonders
 Acts 2:22 says that Jesus was accredited by God 'by miracles, wonders and signs, which God did among you through him.' This was a major thrust and part of Jesus' ministry that clearly continued through the life of the apostles and the early church. Why is this so, and why do we need miracles, signs and wonders? Paul says in 1 Corinthians 2:4-5, "My message and my preaching were not with wise and persuasive words, but with a demonstration of the Spirit's power, so that your faith might not rest on men's wisdom, but on God's power." Paul recognised that many times people

needed to see a demonstration of the power of God. This is necessary for three reasons.

First, it gets people's attention. Second, it reveals something of who God is, shows them what he can do, and tends to wipe away a lot of arguments. Third, as Paul says here, it will cause faith to be in God and his power, instead of in men and their wisdom. There are other ways in which we can demonstrate the gospel, but healing and miracles seemed to be a main approach in the New Testament and is a means that makes us depend on God.

So what are miracles and signs and wonders? A dictionary definition of a miracle would be 'a marvellous event attributed to a supernatural cause.' It is a breaking in of God's activity, which he usually does through one of his servants. It is an act of God that defies what would normally be possible. The Bible of course is full of accounts of miracles from creation onwards: Moses parting the sea, manna in the desert, the conquering of Jericho, Elijah calling down fire, Elisha raising the dead, and of course the whole life of Jesus, and then the acts of his followers (that is just to highlight a small selection).

The Bible uses the term 'signs and wonders' because that is the primary purpose of healings and other miracles. They are to act as a sign to those who are lost, and they are to cause people to wonder, to marvel and to make them consider what God might be saying. The church does not need signs and wonders. If I am driving in my own city, I do not look for signs because I know the way. When I am in a part of the country that I do not know then signs are a great help to me. Christians will experience healing and miracles, but the main point of them is to be a sign to those who do not know the way. John Wimber described signs and wonders as the calling cards of the Kingdom and the catalyst for evangelism.

Types of Miracles and Reactions to them

In the Scriptures, we come across various miraculous phenomena such as healing, the raising of the dead, angelic visitations, casting out of demons, and miracles over nature, including the calming of storms and the multiplication of food. There are several miraculous births recorded, and also miraculous deliverances from prisons and from a lion's den.

We also find varying reactions to these occurrences. At the empty tomb, the appearance of the mighty angel causes the guards to faint like dead men, but he encourages the women not to fear, and releases a message of wonder and joy to them that Jesus has risen from the dead. The people of Israel experienced many miracles in the desert but most of them fell away in unbelief. They became too familiar and took what God did for granted. They allowed their problems to overshadow the wonders of God, letting grumbling rule their hearts. This is a warning for us. Jesus also warned the cities that saw his miracles and failed to respond to him that they were worse off than Sodom and Gomorrah (see Luke 10:10-16). He also said that it was a wicked and adulterous generation that looked for a miraculous sign (Matthew 12:38-39). Yet Jesus did many miracles as signs to the people. What do we make of this? The ones Jesus rebuked were the religious ones, the ones who should have recognised him from the Old Testament prophecies. However, to the crowds whom he described as 'harassed and helpless like sheep without a shepherd,' among them he did many miraculous signs. We should not seek miracles to prove anything or for the sake of a spiritual high, but we should seek them to advance the spread of the Good News of the Kingdom of God.

It is in the book of Acts that we most clearly see the positive effect of miracles, though even there they also at times led to persecution. We will look at some of the passages in that book next.

Exciting witness and Explosive Growth
Evangelism is showing and speaking (that is demonstrating and proclaiming) the Good News of the Kingdom of God and introducing people to the King.

There have been countless methods of evangelism, some of which seemed contrived, awkward, guilt-motivated, and manipulative. These have put many off doing the work of evangelism and may have put many off coming to Jesus. There is another way - a dynamic and natural expression of our lives and believing communities displaying the life, love and power of Christ. Jesus said in Acts 1:8 "you will receive power when the Holy Spirit comes on you; and you will be my witnesses in Jerusalem, and in all Judea and Samaria, and to the ends of the earth."

Is evangelism meant to be terribly hard work with little fruit? On the other hand, might it be an exciting adventure with the Holy Spirit that can lead to much fruit? I think the accounts of the book of Acts suggest it can be the latter.

Imagine a man travelling home from work one day when he witnesses a serious car crash. Firefighters rush to the scene and heroically rescue two people from a burning car. When the man finally gets home, do you think he would have told his family about what he had witnessed? Of course he would, he probably could not wait to relate the whole exciting story to everyone he met. The disciples had witnessed the works and words of Jesus; they had met with the Risen Lord; and now they were seeing the power of his Spirit at work through their lives. All that led to them being compelled to speak of these things: *For we cannot help speaking about what we have seen and heard.* (Acts 4:20)

Acts 2 sees the coming of the Spirit in power with the manifestation (miraculous sign) of the disciples speaking in unknown tongues and others hearing them in their native languages. This was of course a reversal of what happened at the tower of Babel (Genesis 11) where God scattered the peoples and confused their speech. The marvellous sign on this day of Pentecost causes a stir and Peter finds the opportunity to address the crowd. The people listen and are convicted by the Holy Spirit, and many come to the Lord, some 3000 people. We see here the first evidence of explosive growth. A similar pattern develops throughout the next chapters of Acts.

Acts 3 finds Peter and John going to the Temple to pray. They encounter the lame beggar who is appealing for money. They have no money for him but instead give him the healing power of Jesus. The lame man gets to his feet and leaps around praising God, again causing quite a stir. His healing is a sign and a wonder. The people gather to see, and Peter once more takes the opportunity to preach the Good News in explanation of what just took place, that is the demonstration of the Good News of the Kingdom. Once more, many people believe the message and put their faith in Jesus.

The disciples now experience their first serious opposition and are warned not to speak any more about Jesus (Acts 4). They gather together and pray, crying out to God to give them more boldness in the light of these threats, and they ask that the Lord would stretch out his hand to heal. They have already seen and understood that this is a key to giving those clear opportunities and the boldness to make the most of these moments.

Let's move on to Acts 8:4-8 where Philip goes to Samaria. It was as a result of persecution that many of the believers left Jerusalem, and began to fulfill Jesus' command to go to Judea, Samaria and to the ends of the earth. Philip proclaims Christ in this town, and as verse 6 tells us, 'when they saw the miraculous signs he did, they all paid close attention to what he said.' It was the signs and wonders that got people's attention, and caused them to listen carefully and closely to Philip. As many were healed, the result was great joy in that city.

Next, we come across Peter on his travels. In Acts 9:32-43 he goes to Lydda and Joppa where two miraculous signs take place. In Lydda, Peter pronounces healing to a paralytic named Aeneas, who had been bedridden for eight years. Immediately the man gets up and the whole town turns to the Lord. Meanwhile in nearby Joppa a disciple called Tabitha (Dorcas) has just died. The church sends for Peter who comes and enters the house where she had been laid. Following what he saw Jesus do in the home of Jairus, Peter puts the people out (removes the hindrance of unbelief) and he prays. I imagine he asked the Father what he was to do here. Should he, and could he, bring her back to life? Presumably he sensed a 'yes' and he raises the dead woman, and presents her to the people. Word of this spread and many believed in the Lord.

Next, we see the mission activities of Paul. First in Acts 14:8-20 he is in Lystra where he speaks the healing word to a crippled man. It caused quite a stir, with the crowd first wanting to worship Paul and Barnabas, and then in no time wanting to stone them! Miraculous signs can indeed bring a variety of responses, but they do get a response.

In Acts 19:11-20 Paul is in Ephesus where he finds a small band of disciples, who after Paul baptises them and lays hands on them, receive the Holy Spirit and prophesy. Paul spends considerable time there teaching, and verse 11 notes that he did *'extraordinary miracles.'* Again, there is a stirring and a shifting in the city with a massive display of repentance, and the word of the Lord spreading widely. This does not come without some reaction and a riot ensues in that city.

Our final stop is on the island of Malta in Acts 28:1-10. Paul finds himself there due to a shipwreck, and two main miraculous signs occur. First, Paul is bitten by a snake but suffers no ill effects. This sign causes the people to wonder. Second, Paul brings healing to the chief official's father who was suffering from dysentery. As word gets out, all the sick on the island come to be healed.

We observe a clear pattern in the book of Acts – a miraculous happening takes place; this acts as a sign and a wonder to the people who then are ready to listen to the message of the Kingdom of God. There is a significant response - often of many coming to faith – and also on some occasions this is accompanied by persecution. The early church seemed quite happy with all of this and were certainly not put off by the opposition (see Acts 5:41-42; 1 Corinthians 16:8-9).

Taking Opportunities and Giving Answers
While the book of Acts demonstrates the powerful and effective witness of the early church, the letters of the apostles in the New Testament have little to say on the matter of evangelism. They do not give much instruction on how to 'do' evangelism. This would

suggest that the early believers just got on with it – it was the natural thing to do - it was spontaneous. There are two verses though that give some interesting insights:

Colossians 4:5 *Be wise in the way you act toward outsiders; make the most of every opportunity.*

1 Peter 3:15 *But in your hearts set apart Christ as Lord. Always be prepared to give an answer to everyone who asks you to give the reason for the hope that you have. But do this with gentleness and respect.*

These verses instruct us to be wise, gentle and respectful in our conduct as we engage with people. The first text assumes there will be opportunities, and the second assumes we will be asked something.

So two important questions to ask are:
   1) What creates opportunities?   2) What causes questions to be asked?
From what we have already discovered from the book of Acts, it is evident that healings and other miracles gave definite and wonderful opportunities to share the message. Likewise some sort of demonstration of the Spirit's power, or of a truly Spirit filled and led life, will cause people to ask questions. It is important not to be too quick in trying to tell people the answer. Let them ask the question first! Sometimes in their enthusiasm, Christians are attempting to give an answer to a question nobody is asking. Part of gentleness and respect is to listen to people and listen well.

A while ago, I spoke at a church where a number of people received prayer for healing. I received an e-mail a few days later to say that one of the women there had been healed of a painful hip problem that had required her to wear one built up shoe. Everything was now in line and she could wear two flat shoes. Then the message continued saying that her work colleagues were amazed at what had happened. It was a miraculous sign and wonder into her workplace, which would create a glorious opportunity.

The Present Day Need

We have had the privilege of having Brother Yun, the Chinese church leader known as the 'Heavenly Man,' with us on two occasions. He has told us that around 80% of the vast numbers of people coming to faith in Jesus in China today are first drawn by a miracle in their life or someone close to them. People need to and want to see if the Gospel works. They want to know if Jesus can make a difference in their life.

It has been interesting over the last few years to experience very real interest in what we do from members of the press. Several local and even national newspapers have carried favourable accounts of healings and stories about our ministry. In the northerly Orkney Islands, both local papers ran a story containing the testimony of a woman healed from a chronic fatigue condition. The paper showed a photograph of her beside the wheelchair that she no longer required. Her testimony was reported word for word, clearly displaying Jesus as the healer. We are given the clear impression that the world is just waiting for the church to release the genuine, life transforming power of God to them. People are fed up with hearing hollow words and empty promises from all sorts of sectors of society. Many are looking for what will deal with their pain, their needs, or their confusion. They need to witness and experience the signs and wonders of the Kingdom of God.

An older lady came in to one of our Glasgow rooms. She was suffering from osteoarthritis, which caused much pain in her joints. She had no church connection and this was her first experience of receiving prayer for healing. As often happens, some tears rolled down her cheeks as she sensed the loving, peaceful presence of God. She felt good afterwards, and came back the following week to report that since receiving prayer she had experienced no pain whatsoever, and was even telling people that God had healed her. She then told us that she had been praying all week, asking God if he could forgive her for not giving him any place in her life. We made the most of the opportunity, shared the Good News message with her, and she turned in faith to the Lord and received his salvation.

We have witnessed this happen on numerous occasions and are seeing the number of instances increase all the time. Releasing healing as a sign and wonder has great affect. It was what happened frequently in the early church leading to explosive growth, and is what can happen today with similar results. We have really only just begun. Now it is time to enter into the so much more that God has for us.

Chapter 6

An Explosion of the Miraculous

Everyone was filled with awe, and many wonders and miraculous signs were done by the apostles Acts 2:43

Following Jesus is about many things – developing Christ-like character and the inner purity of the heart (see Matthew 5-7); growing in a loving community; growing in relationship with the Father; expressing this relationship in prayer and much more. Miracles were a large feature in the life and ministry of Jesus, and must be fully re-discovered as the experience of the church today. Jesus' birth through to his glorious resurrection and ascension was an explosion of the miraculous workings of God.

As I sought the Lord for his word to us at the start of 2007 I sensed the Holy Spirit speak these words to me: *'I will move you from an exploration of the miraculous into an explosion of the miraculous.'* I have never found it a good idea to argue with what God says to me, and I certainly was not going to argue with this! It was true that for some time we had been exploring around in the miraculous dimension, and had seen some amazing things happen. How we would get from there to this explosion was probably not my business at that stage – he said he would move us there. Since then we have seen a definite increase in miraculous healings, and I believe I have seen some of the keys for getting to that place. It does feel like we have just seen a few hand grenades go off and are still waiting for the bigger blasts of his power.

As I highlighted in the previous chapter, the purpose of miracles is to enable the church to reach the lost people of our generation effectively. Jesus had an expectation of a harvest (see Matthew 9:37-38; Luke 10:2 and John 4:35); it was workers he was requiring. A harvest is preceded by first fruits, and I believe we have seen the first fruits of this harvest. That is a guarantee that the full harvest is coming. It is not automatic though, and we cannot lie back and just wait, but need to respond and be those workers whom Jesus sends out in the power of his Spirit. There are some who see this in the Spirit and prepare, but they are the few. Most of God's people need to see the signs of the fruit before they take seriously the urgency of the time and the task.

Healing the Eyes
Helen received an amazing healing from the Lord a little while ago. Some time before this, her eye was damaged, resulting in dryness in the eyes, which an expert told her would require her to apply gel to lubricate the eyes six times a day for the rest of her life! Helen received prayer ministry, and afterwards saw what seemed like a small stitch come out from her eye. Since then she has had no problems, even going into shopping centres, where the lights and air conditioning used to cause considerable irritation. Not only does God heal physical eye conditions, but also he wants to heal our inner sight, so we can see what his Spirit is doing in the land. He also wants us to keep

the right focus. When I asked Brother Yun what he saw was the main problem of the Western church, he replied that it seemed to be a lack of focus. He said that the persecution in China gives them focus. We need to be focused on the main task of making disciples.

As God is beginning to move us in this direction, he has graciously released an increase in the number of healings among us. Here is a small selection:

A lady went for prayer for ME (chronic fatigue syndrome) at the Stirling rooms. She has been healed and no longer needs the stick she used for walking. At a recent healing meeting, someone left a walking stick behind! Then we were given a 'redundant' walking stick at our conference when a woman had her knee healed. We are beginning a collection of walking sticks at our office!

Another person received prayer for her hearing recently, and left the room with her two hearing aids in her handbag. At a recent training event, a woman who received prayer at our 'demonstration session,' testified that as the Holy Spirit came on her the pain she had been experiencing for years left her. She testified at our conference a few weeks later that since then she has felt like a new person, and her friends have been commenting on the change.

Another lady wrote to us saying, *"I came to Healing Rooms at a time when I was feeling very low. I had been diagnosed with vascular disease in my forties, and statistically the long-term outlook was not good. I felt resigned to my fate of a premature death, although I tried very hard to stay positive. When I came to the Healing Rooms, the team prayed for my physical healing and my emotional healing from past events in my life. It was a peaceful and loving encounter. Not long after this, I had to attend hospital for tests and they told me that these showed no evidence of this disease. I have been discharged and look forward to living a productive and full life."*

And just the other day we received this testimony from one of our volunteers. *"Having come of age! (50) I was given an appointment for a mammogram. A few days later, a letter arrived saying further x-rays were needed. These revealed a small lump which they did a biopsy on that same day. Two weeks later I was told the lump should be removed, so a hospital appointment was made for the operation.*
At the Healing Rooms, I asked that they would agree with me in prayer that when I went to the hospital they wouldn't be able to find anything. So when I went down to x-ray again on the day of my operation, after nearly two hours of searching with many different angles on the x-ray machine, they said they could not find the lump. So I was sent home with no operation. Praise God. The doctor said that in over 20 years of doing this she had never had this happen before."

These accounts are just a few of the first fruits that we are witnessing, and most importantly alongside this, we are seeing a growing number of people coming to faith.

Doing what could only happen through the power of God

There is much of what we do in our lives and the activity of our churches that might easily carry on the same whether God was in it or not. Even some of the right things we do, and should continue to do, like acts of kindness, could be done without the Holy Spirit's assistance. I have made it an aim that in our ministry we seek to do things that are impossible without God working in and through us. Then there is no doubt that the glory must go to him. We are not called to be nice people – we are called to be Spirit empowered world changers. We will not always be popular but we will make a difference.

The Road to the Miraculous

What is the road God moves us down to get to the place of miracles? As you can imagine it is not an easy road but one that tests us, shapes us and teaches us many things. The road in my experience and what I see in Scripture has four avenues.

1. The Desert Avenue: In Luke 4:1 Jesus, being full of the Holy Spirit is led, driven even, by the same Spirit into the desert. He spends time there fasting and praying, and undergoes a time of serious testing and temptation, which he overcomes with the truth of God's Word. We notice in Luke 4:14 that Jesus returns *'in the power of the Spirit.'* There is, I believe, a deliberate distinction in the descriptions that Luke uses. Something occurred in Jesus while in that wilderness. As John Lake noted, when Jesus went into the desert he had the Spirit, when he came out of the desert the Spirit had him. A life that is fully given over to the Holy Spirit is a life that will move in his genuine power.

There are two other salient points about the desert experience. First, Jesus fasts and prays over an extended period of time. This is a key to overcoming the weakness of the flesh and breaking through into a new dimension of living. Second, Jesus resists every temptation to prove himself or for personal aggrandizement, and submits to the revealed words of Scripture.

There are four areas I focus on in my life in seeking this growth and breakthrough: to study and obey God's Word; to practice spiritual disciplines – prayer, fasting, solitude etc; to receive revelation from the Holy Spirit; and to have life changing encounters with God. I believe the first two, which we can choose to practice, position us for the other two, which are dependent on God. In the desert, Jesus demonstrated and overcame the enemy with his knowledge of, and obedience to, the Word of God. He practiced spiritual discipline as he fasted, building on the revelation and experience following his baptism.

We can experience the desert or wilderness roads in many ways. Some of these are of our own doing, but God can still bring redemptive purposes from those if we turn to him and submit to his ways. Some are like Jesus' experience where we are driven there by God. It is good not to despise these times or seek to end them too early, but let them work in us the good and pleasing will of God. It is the place Moses learned to observe the presence of God in a burning bush, and David learned to lean on God more fully. We need to learn the desert's lessons if we are to be readied for the miraculous dimension.

2. The Storm Avenue: In Luke 8:22 – 56 we find a series of miraculous events and works. A raging storm is stilled; a hopelessly insane and demonised man is cured; a sick woman is healed by touching the edge of Jesus' cloak; and a twelve-year-old girl is raised from the dead. Its awesome stuff and it starts with a storm.

One day Jesus said to his disciples, "Let's go over to the other side of the lake." So they got into a boat and set out. As they sailed, he fell asleep. A squall came down on the lake, so that the boat was being swamped, and they were in great danger. The disciples went and woke him, saying, "Master, Master, we're going to drown!"   He got up and rebuked the wind and the raging waters; the storm subsided, and all was calm. "Where is your faith?" he asked his disciples. In fear and amazement they asked one another, "Who is this? He commands even the winds and the water, and they obey him. Luke 8:22-25

Before Jesus got to the other side, where we see him demonstrating his power and authority over demons, disease and death, he and his disciples had to get through quite a storm. The disciples, some of whom were experienced fishermen, were terrified and woke Jesus while in fear for their lives. Now Jesus rebukes their lack of faith, which we might feel is a little harsh. However, he had been training them in the ways of divine power and authority, and maybe expected that they should have learned to speak to the storm themselves.

There are storms that hinder us moving on in God's purposes and we need to speak to them. There are storms sent from God to re-direct us, like with Jonah, and we need to listen and alter course. However, I think there is an even more crucial understanding of this event. Notice Jesus had said, *'Let's go over to the other side.'* Jesus intended and had announced that that was where they were going. The enemy may have instigated a furious squall but he was not going to stop them crossing the lake. Jesus slept in the midst of it, and I believe wants us to learn to sleep through such storms, as we rest in the security and certainty of God's word to us. The more we have pressed in to new ground over the years the more we have encountered storms, sometimes with regular predictability. Fear cries out for the storm to be stilled, but there are times for faith to come to the fore and simply state 'we are going to the other side.'

To enter the arena of the miraculous works of God we need to learn to trust him completely through the storms. As we cross to the other side – the new arena of breakthrough - having rested in God through the enemy's challenges, we are being equipped to deal with the legions of demons, the incurable diseases and even the power of death. In the desert, we learn to depend on God's Word and come out in renewed power. In the storm, we learn to rest in God's promises and come through with increased authority. (We shall look more at the place of power and authority in the next chapter).

3. The Desperation Avenue: I have heard it said that in many places around the world where God has moved in great power and brought real transformation, a key factor in this has been desperation. We get desperate when we realise how crucial it is to have God's power move among us and out from us. The Spirit of God is the one who initiates this desperate cry within us. It is a cry we discover in a number of the Psalms:

Restore us again, O God our Saviour …
Will you not revive us again….
Show us your unfailing love, O LORD
And grant us your salvation. Psalm 85:4-7

We have seen and felt this cry, and witnessed what has happened in response. Last year a number of our leaders were away for two days. On the Friday night, after our scheduled meetings, it seemed right that we stay up and cry out to God for greater breakthrough. We got on our faces for a couple of hours crying out with deep desperation. There came a point where we sensed it was done. The next day, as I ministered to and prayed over the group, I experienced a level of anointing I had never quite known before. Since then we have also observed an increase of fruitfulness in many of our rooms.

On another occasion, in one of our rooms, the leaders sensed the stirring of the Spirit to have their team all get down on their knees and cry out loudly. They even roared into the floor. When they opened to the public that morning a woman came in who received a wonderful miraculous healing, and whose testimony brought many more people who in turn were touched powerfully by God. This woman was suffering from a lung condition that meant she had to be on oxygen, and if she was ever able to get out it was in a wheelchair. She needed a lung transplant but had been too ill to receive one, and was only expected to live for a short time. As the team ministered to her, she felt God's presence go through her lungs and was immediately healed.

Breakthrough miracles, which can open up new territory, will come to those who travel the road of desperation.

4. The Service Avenue: Stephen was a man who served tables (Acts 6:1-6), but quickly became a man who 'did great wonders and miraculous signs among the people' (Acts 6:8). Jesus said that he came not to be served but to serve (Mark 10:45). How much more should we all be willing to serve? I find this arena of service is very revealing about the character and potential of a person. Those who are faithful with small tasks can be trusted with greater ones. Those who serve quietly, in the unseen and unrecognised places, are the ones God will raise up to the realm of miracles. Those who are willing to take the lowly seat are invited up to the top of the table and vice versa. I believe it was Martin Luther King who said, 'Anyone can be great, because anyone can serve.'

Breakthrough Miracles
A miracle, for example of healing, may occur, and while it is wonderful for the person involved, it may not have a much wider impact. There are other miracles that take place that can have a wide impact. These are vital for reaching our communities and nations. What do breakthrough miracles do?

1. They break and release something in the heavenly realm. This seemed to be the case in Acts 19 when Paul was in Ephesus.
2. They release an increased level of faith in us – they extend our faith boundary. They release expectant faith for more.
3. They release a testimony on earth, which in turn releases the prophetic spirit that declares that this can happen again.

Matthew 15:21-39 shows us the process of such breakthrough. The Canaanite woman comes to Jesus pleading for her daughter whose need is desperate. Because of her pressing through the obstacles, she gets the breakthrough for her daughter.

In the next verses (29-31), we read of multitudes coming and large numbers are healed from all manner of conditions. This may not be directly related here but it illustrates what can happen. When one healing takes place, people hear about it and come seeking healing for themselves. After the healings, the crowds gather around Jesus and he miraculously feeds them. The Canaanite woman had asked just for crumbs from the table, but Jesus is able to make bread abound for a multitude. He does not send anyone away hungry.

There are certain miracles that will happen that will have a far-reaching effect. As we pursue the Lord, as the Canaanite woman did, with great perseverance we can witness such breakthrough. She sought the Lord, refusing to be put off by his silence or the dismissive remarks of the disciples. She did not take offence, but pressed in out of desperation to see her daughter made well.

Releasing the Backlog of Miracles
God is not slow to answer, and it is his desire to demonstrate his Kingdom on the earth. He continues to do this, as he has done before, through miraculous signs and wonders. The problem is always on the earth, not in heaven, and there has been a lot of interference blocking the miracles getting through to their destination. Sure, the enemy takes every chance he gets to block things, but the real culprit as always is the unbelief of God's people. As we rise up in expectant faith, casting aside fear and pressing through in desperation, I believe we can see the release of the miracles that have been coming from heaven's throne but have been held up on the way. Like a dam bursting we will see an explosion of the miraculous break out into our towns and cities, bringing a great shaking and a clear demonstration of the person of Christ Jesus. As it comes, we must remember what it is for: to introduce the many to the

one who can save, heal and deliver and bring them into new and full life.

Chapter 7
Appointed and Anointed to be Fruitful

You did not choose me, but I chose you and appointed you to go and bear fruit—fruit that will last John 15:16

I am a bit of a football fan (that is soccer for my American friends), and as a small boy it was an ambition of mine to play professionally for one of the big clubs. Well it is good to have dreams even if they do not all come to fruition. Now that I am largely past the age of playing, I content myself to sit back and watch others. The thing about the Christian life, of course, is that there are not meant to be any spectators – you all get to play in the team. I am a bit of a cricket fan too, which is unusual for a Scotsman, and used to play for a local club in Glasgow as a youngster. I remember travelling to an away match one time, only to find out when we got there that I was the 12th man (there's 11 in a team so in other words I got to sit at the side and watch). I was very disappointed and maybe still need some deeper healing! The point is it is much more fun to participate.

The strange thing I have found about some Christians is they seem content to be spectators and watch others participate. I have always preferred to be involved and to be active. I have to say I much prefer preaching than listening to someone else preach! Most preachers are the same I am sure. However, it is not just about personal preference here. Jesus calls all his followers to be active and participate together in his team. This chapter is all about how we can all play our part.

The Fruit of Friendship:

My command is this: Love each other as I have loved you. Greater love has no one than this, that he lay down his life for his friends. You are my friends if you do what I command. I no longer call you servants, because a servant does not know his master's business. Instead, I have called you friends, for everything that I learned from my Father I have made known to you. You did not choose me, but I chose you and appointed you to go and bear fruit—fruit that will last. Then the Father will give you whatever you ask in my name. This is my command: Love each other.
John 15:12-17

This passage speaks about our appointment to be fruitful. It is an appointment that arises out of friendship. It is an awesome fact that Jesus calls us friends, not slaves; that we are chosen and appointed. This releases us from two of our greatest struggles in life.

(1) From the fear of failure. Most of us have at some point battled against the fear of failing, and even of being a failure. We have inside us a God created desire to live a significant life. That is a good thing. It gets distorted by the sinful nature, and is reduced to

toil and striving out of a sense of insecurity that can drive us to prove our worth. Jesus' friendship, which he has initiated with us, frees us from our insecurity. He then calls us simply to abide in him (John 15:5), the result of which is the bearing of fruit in our lives.

(2) From being in the dark. Again, many people have lived life unsure of themselves and unclear about what to do. Jesus' friendship means he makes known to us all that he has learned from the Father. That is a lot and involves a lifetime of listening to him. This revelation results in us being able to engage in the fruitful activities of God's will, instead of wasting time doing our own thing.

The friendship we have with Jesus draws us into intimacy and leads to fruitfulness. So two amazing fruits of this friendship that these verses speak about are:
   (1) Revelation of all the Father has made known (v15).
   (2) Answers to our prayers (v17) because we ask in line with the revelation of his will.
Another key in this relationship is to love one another; after all, we are all his friends. The essential matter for us is to develop this friendship with Jesus.

The Time is Now: Opportunities and Possibilities
This present time is full of opportunity with every day holding out to us possibilities for Kingdom works and witness. Stephen, one of our volunteers, shared with us the other week that he had popped into a large supermarket for a few groceries. His general practice

120

is to be asking the Father on the way if there is anyone he wants him to notice and speak to, or offer prayer to. He noticed a woman struggling to pick up a bag of sugar, so he approached her and engaged in a little conversation. The woman told Stephen that she found it difficult to pick things up because of the arthritis affecting her joints. Stephen offered prayer, which she accepted. We find many people are very open to receive prayer in all sorts of locations. As he prayed, the power of the Holy Spirit clearly started to affect the woman. Stephen went out to his car to get a Healing Room card for her, and when he found her again she was still clearly under the influence of the Spirit! There are opportunities everywhere.

Indeed, there is great spiritual hunger in this time that is evident through the plethora of new age and other spiritualities that abound. This is not something that we should rue or bemoan. This is time for the church to rise up and reveal the true and powerful spirituality of the living God. Unfortunately, many in the church are playing catch up.

For some years now, we have been taking stalls at psychic fairs, where our teams pray with and prophesy to many people there. A good number have come to faith in Jesus and started to follow him. Further to this, some of our people have developed a ministry called *Light and Life*, which exists to provide a demonstration of true Christian spirituality, showing God's love and power in a creative and culturally relevant way. (See www.Lightlife.org.uk) The evenings they run, often in coffee shops or hotels, are packed out, and we hear testimonies of people coming to faith, being healed or having significant encounters with God.

The opportunities abound, the possibilities seem endless and the harvest is plentiful; it is just the workers we need. The Body of Christ needs to be released and made ready for action.

Releasing the Body of Christ
Our vision is to raise up ordinary believers to do extraordinary things. When Jimmy first came to the Healing Rooms in Paisley he was a very unwell man, and his yellowish complexion was a tell tale sign that his liver was not functioning properly. Strong medication for a heart condition had been damaging his liver over a period of time and tests at the hospital confirmed this. The bad news was that Jimmy was told that the damage was irreparable, and the liver would not regenerate. After receiving prayer for healing a few times, Jimmy began to feel much better and his colour markedly changed. Subsequent tests at the hospital showed that his liver was now fully functioning once more. Jimmy was filled with the Holy Spirit in a completely new way, subsequently attended our training course and became a volunteer in a Healing Room. Now well into his seventies he takes delight in praying for the sick.

You Give Them Something to Eat
In Luke 9:12-17 we read the account of the feeding of the 5,000. When and through whom did this great miracle occur? The text does not actually state when the food multiplied. Was it as Jesus broke it or was it

as the disciples distributed it? Either way, the point is Jesus told his disciples to feed the crowd. There are many hungry people today looking for the true bread but not knowing where to look. The church, often seen as a lumbering institution, does not appear in the eyes of many of them as having the answer. The disciples suggested a reasonable and rational solution for the people's hunger – send them to the surrounding villages. But Jesus was looking to stretch their faith to see the miraculous possibility. We are not to be limited by what we possess in the natural, but stretched by our potential in the Spirit. Jesus teaches his disciples four lessons here:

1. Accept your God given responsibility – you feed them; you heal them; you overcome the power of the enemy. He has provided the necessary means; he expects us to handle the necessary distribution.

2. Organise your approach – divide the 5,000 into groups of 50 (v14). The needs around us can appear overwhelming, so it is vital to know where to begin and how to proceed, otherwise we can end up talking but doing nothing. Simply start somewhere and then proceed little by little.

3. Put what you have in the hands of Jesus – they only had some fish and loaves, but when put in Jesus' hands, where it is broken and blessed; it multiplies as it is given away. God asked Moses what he had in his hand. It was an ordinary,

everyday staff. Yet God enabled Moses to wield that staff with miraculous authority over Egypt.

4. Expect miracles and multiplication. Why not?

This is the time for the whole Body of Christ to awaken and arise into the potential that each member carries. There may be a few who seem to have a special anointing, but the rest of us are not meant to sit back admiring and applauding them. If anything, they should inspire us to do the same. We all can because we all contain the seeds of faith and the presence of the Holy Spirit. It is time to have a go! I love the story of Jonathan and his armour bearer in 1 Samuel 14:1-15. Despite the rest of the army languishing in a depressed state, and despite being significantly outnumbered by the Philistines, Jonathan suggests to his armour bearer that they make a daring attack on the enemy outpost. They have a go saying, *'perhaps the Lord will act on our behalf.'* Their courage is rewarded, and they conquer the outpost. This act leads to a routing of the whole Philistine army as Saul and the Israelite army eventually spring to life.

In the church today we need some very ordinary heroes to have a go, doing what Jesus said we could, and who knows, such action might stir up many others out of their slumber. One of our volunteers in Edinburgh had a go one day. He encountered a man in a wheelchair in the street and approached him offering to pray for him. At first, the man refused and even unleashed a torrent of criticism towards the church. The young man sensed God tell him to just listen and wait. He did and then again offered prayer. This time the wheelchair bound man accepted. God touched him powerfully, and later he came to the local Healing Room where he got out the wheelchair and came to faith in Christ.

Jesus has given us permission to go and proclaim the Good News of the Kingdom, to heal the sick and drive out demons. We need to seize the opportunities and not give in to any fear. We must go into the enemy's camp, into the darkest places, not fearing contamination but instead looking to spread the infectious love of God. Under the law, contact with lepers made you unclean, but when Jesus touches lepers the leper becomes clean! He sends us – it is his idea. He has empowered us and given us authority. Let us look at those two keys now.

Power and Authority

On a Sabbath Jesus was teaching in one of the synagogues, and a woman was there who had been crippled by a spirit for eighteen years. She was bent over and could not straighten up at all. When Jesus saw her, he called her forward and said to her, "Woman, you are set free from your infirmity." Then he put his hands on her, and immediately she straightened up and praised God. Luke 13:10-13

Here we find a woman who *'could not raise herself up'* (NKJV), and who had been in this state, crippled by a spirit for 18 years. We see Jesus actions towards her; this is also how he acts towards us, and how we are to minister to others. Jesus healed her through the word of authority and the act of power.

1. **Jesus saw her** (v12): He noticed her and saw her condition, including its root cause. He also 'saw' her free in the Spirit before anything happened.
2. **He calls her forward**: He calls her out of her bondage; out from the place she was trapped and stuck in. He's always calling people forward out of their past and into the 'more' of God and his Kingdom.
3. **He authorises her healing and freedom** (v12b). He spoke in faith the word of authority. He called in the present what was about to come – 'you are set free'. He loosed on earth what had been loosed (released, permitted) in heaven (see Matt. 18:18 NASB). So too, he speaks into us loosing the purposes of heaven in our lives.
4. **He touched her with power:** When he did, she immediately straightened up and praised God. He spoke the **word** then did the **work** (touch), which led to the **wonder.** As he touches us, he straightens us up into a true God-ward relationship, not bent towards any other thing.

Therefore, we can minister healing by seeing people and seeing the condition and the cause; and what God wants to do with them through the potential they have in Christ. We can call people forward, move them on, and speak to them with authority releasing the will of God from heaven onto the earth. We can be infused with power from on high so that as we touch people the power of God will flow through us into them.

The Power of the Spirit
Jesus told his followers to wait in Jerusalem until they were *'clothed with power from on high.'* (Luke 24:49) This is what we require. The primary purpose of the coming of the Spirit is to anoint us with power to be witnesses of Jesus in the world. We are to be continuously filled with the Spirit (Ephesians 5:18) and operate in the gifts of the Spirit. The true gift we are given is the Holy Spirit himself. That is the gift that we are to stir up in ourselves. He is the Gift of God, who can then distribute whatever gift we need in any given situation. In our ministry, we do not look for people who 'have the gift of healing' as if it is their possession that few others have. We look for people who are acknowledging and partnering with the gift of the Holy Spirit. He will release the necessary healing gift through them.

What are the Gifts of the Spirit?
They are gifts of grace; manifestations of the Spirit; and ministries of the Spirit. They are given to aid communication and give us power to make Jesus known. They are also tools for building up the Body of Christ.

Types of gifts:
Revelation gifts – they reveal something: knowledge, wisdom, distinguishing spirits.
Utterance gifts – these say something: prophecy, tongues and interpretation.

Power gifts – these ones do something: faith, miracles, healing.

Who are the gifts for?
They are for the whole Body of Christ, that is all in the Body, together in the Body. It is about the Body, not individuals. There are some common misconceptions about the gifts that I notice in the churches:

1. An over-emphasis on individualism, whereas Scripture mostly speaks of you (plural) and a corporate anointing. We are not to operate in isolation, but are to value each other in interdependence and operate in dependence on God.
2. People ask 'What's **MY** gift?' As if you have it in a possessive sense and find your value in it. Your value is being in Christ not in your giftedness. Gifts are given as the Spirit determines and benefit us all. Your value is in being a child of God. If you are open to him then all kinds of gifts can flow through you. The gifts are for the Body and for each of us in the Body.
3. Only those with the gift can operate in that area – e.g. healing. We are all sent to heal the sick (Luke 9 and 10). It is about having the Gift, i.e. the Holy Spirit, then letting him flow through us as he wills, flowing with others and welcoming the gifting in others.

We should seek to develop and wear a spiritual 'tool belt' through our relationship with the Holy Spirit, and then he can give us whatever tool we need when we need it. The various gifts can all work together in any situation. Tongues is said to be the least of the gifts (this is often emphasised by people who are not very keen on tongues, but Paul's words are not meant to be dismissive of this gift). It is often a good starting point, like a gateway into the other gifts. Tongues is probably the most offensive gift to the human mind and to our pride. At first, it does not appear to be of any earthly use. Of course it is, as it builds up our inner man, and I have found this gift to be vital in intercessory prayer.

Words of knowledge, distinguishing of spirits or prophecy can all play a hugely helpful part in healing ministry. I was preaching in a church one Sunday where someone in the congregation had a 'word' about a pain in the left knee that he believed God was healing. I responded to this, having had a continual problem of pain in that knee caused by wear and tear from my football playing days. Often at night, especially after days when I had stood a lot, the searing pain would feel like a hot iron burning through the knee. Anyway, I received prayer and since that day, some years ago now, I have never again experienced any pain in my knee.

On another occasion, I was preaching in a different church. This time I sensed the Lord say he was going to heal spinal conditions. Several responded and received the laying on of hands for healing. The pastor told me a few days later, that one woman who had suffered years of back pain, felt that morning as if a hand went inside her back and manipulated her spine.

She was now pain free for the first time in years. The operation of these 'word gifts' releases faith for healing to be more easily received.

Operating in the gifts:
God wants us to receive the gift of the Holy Spirit and be filled continually with the Spirit. He wants us to be released in ministry; equipped and empowered with the gifts of the Spirit.

Here are some simple steps to receiving and acting:
1. Desire the gifts – 1 Corinthians14:1
2. Humble yourself – James 4:6
3. Remove any blockages in your life – James 4:7-10
4. Ask – Luke 11:9-13
5. Believe – Mark 11:24
6. Receive – John 20:22; Acts 1:8
7. Act, put what you receive into action straight away – Matthew 10:6-8
8. Keep on stirring up the gift – 2 Timothy 1:6

The Authority of Christ
What do we see in the Bible about this subject of authority? Jesus has been granted authority by the Father – John 17:2; Matthew 9:6. Jesus was under the Father's authority so he could exercise proper authority. Jesus teaching was recognised as having authority – Mark 1:27. Jesus received all authority in heaven and on earth – Matthew 28:18; Philippians 2:6-11: Ephesians 1:20 -23. Jesus will eventually hand back his authority to God the Father – 1 Corinthians 15:24-28

Our Authority In and Under Christ:
Jesus gave authority to his disciples to heal the sick and drive out demons – Matthew 10:1; Luke 9:1.
Our authority is dependent on our position as children of God and ambassadors of Christ – John 1:12; 2 Corinthians 5:20. We represent him, that is we represent him today.
Our authority requires submission and continuous relationship with Jesus – John 15:5.
We must beware of the wrong use of authority – Matthew 20:25-28.

In the beginning, God gave man authority to rule over creation as his representative. When man sinned, he lost this authority allowing Satan to usurp it. In fact, man gave Satan his rights to rule. Of course, God intervened many times throughout history, often in response to the cries of his people. Finally, Jesus came. He was the one who was without sin and therefore not subject to the authority of Satan or death. When he laid down his life on the cross, death took the one it had no rights to, and its power was vanquished. Jesus burst forth from the grave having dealt with sin and triumphing over all the powers of darkness. He now has all authority in heaven and earth – that is absolutely conclusive. Satan does not waste his efforts challenging that any more.

Jesus regained the authority that man lost in the Garden of Eden, but even more crucially, he has delegated that authority back to his church. This is where the enemy comes back in with his challenge, attempting to deceive us from realising what Christ has bestowed on us. Our call is to rule with him and to have dominion over the works of the evil one. It is therefore also pivotal that we not only understand that this authority has been delegated to us once more, but that we start to exercise it. Having authority is of no use unless we employ it. It is our task to speak out the purposes of God; to pronounce his truth; and to loose the activities of heaven on the earth.

The Anointing

Jesus has given us power and authority. For these to flow in our lives we need the anointing of the Holy Spirit. To anoint means to smear with oil. This oil of God is what makes everything that he has given us work properly. When I was a student, I had an old car that had seen better days. However, it worked. It had the power in its engine to move the wheels to get me where I wanted to go. I had the authority to drive having passed my test a few years beforehand. However, this car developed a problem that meant the oil was not getting to where it needed to in the engine. Eventually the car came to a halt. Without the anointing of the Holy Spirit in our lives and ministry, everything can come to a grinding halt. We need to keep receiving the steady flow of his anointing in our lives and on all we do.

It is important to understand that though God may give his anointing to those who ask, the effectiveness of that anointing will depend on where it lands. We need to cultivate a heart after God so that the anointing finds good ground to land on that will produce much fruit.

Getting started and Becoming More Active

Maybe this is all new to you. If so, now is a good time to get started doing the works of the Kingdom that God prepared beforehand for you to do. If you have already got going then it is time to get more active. There is a harvest waiting for us. Here are some practical pointers:

1. Pray and ask God to fill you afresh with his Holy Spirit and release his anointing on your life.
2. Attend any appropriate training courses that would help equip you.
3. Link up with those who are already seeing the sick healed and producing the fruit of Kingdom works.
4. Start looking for opportunities. Train your mind to think that way through the activities of your day.
5. Listen to the prompts of the Holy Spirit.
6. Step out – have a go!

Finally, here are some simple steps in how to get going praying for people, in church services or out on the street, or anywhere else for that matter.

1. Explain what you are going to do. If you think you may lay hands on them, let them know why you will do this, and then do it in a sensitive manner. Help them to relax and be prepared to receive from God. Explain anything you might do such as praying in tongues.

2. Pray simply and naturally. Do not use religious talk and Christian jargon. Do not pray in a way that implies you are passing any judgement on their condition. Simply invite the Lord to touch them, heal them or do whatever is needed. Trust God to do it.

3. See what happens and respond to it. If they start to experience something, for example heat or they begin to fall down, reassure them that this is alright, and that it is a sign of God at work. Bless what you see the Father doing (as John Wimber used to say).

4. Point them toward Jesus as Lord and Saviour. As they experience something of God's power in their life, explain that this comes from a real, personal God who loves them and longs to bring them into relationship with himself. However, do not push too much. They may experience God's power or even healing, but not yet be ready to commit their life to Christ. This may be just one step in several that are often needed before true conversion. Beware of trying to pick unripe fruit.

Following Jesus, and doing what he did, is really quite thrilling. He has appointed us - meaning he has set us in place. He has also anointed us so his power and authority can be released through our touch and words. There are loads of people waiting to receive what you have to give them. 'Freely you have received, freely give' (Matthew 10:8).

Chapter 8

Living in the Spirit of Generosity

"Do not judge, and you will not be judged. Do not condemn, and you will not be condemned. Forgive, and you will be forgiven. Give, and it will be given to you. A good measure, pressed down, shaken together and running over, will be poured into your lap. For with the measure you use, it will be measured to you."
Luke 6:37-38

The ministry of healing has much to do with the anointing of power and authority. There is another essential factor though that is maybe not so obvious. We discover this in one of the features of the early church that we have only alluded to so far: extreme generosity.

All the believers were one in heart and mind. No one claimed that any of his possessions was his own, but they shared everything they had. With great power the apostles continued to testify to the resurrection of the Lord Jesus, and much grace was upon them all. There were no needy persons among them. For from time to time those who owned lands or houses sold them, brought the money from the sales and put it at the apostles' feet, and it was distributed to anyone as he had need. Joseph, a Levite from Cyprus, whom the apostles called Barnabas (which means Son of Encouragement), sold a field he owned and brought the money and put it at the apostles' feet (Acts 4:32-37).

What is generosity?
Generosity might be defined as readiness or liberality in giving; freedom from meanness or smallness of mind or character; largeness or fullness. It has much more to do with the spirit of our minds than just giving money. Of course, willingness to give money is one of the most accurate signals of how generous a person is in their heart.

What does generosity do?
It releases people and releases circumstances. It frees us up to get into the flow of giving and receiving. It liberates people to become more than they are, as the capacity of their minds and hearts are expanded. Generosity brings life and transforms community. It has a powerful effect on relationships. Generosity coming from our lives brings generosity into our lives – 'forgive and you will be forgiven; give and it will be given to you.'

The Generosity of God (Romans 8:32; Ephesians 1:7-8)
God is amazingly generous. He has sometimes been misrepresented as mean and withholding, as if we have to 'twist his arm' in prayer to get anything. Not so! He lavishes his goodness on us; he longs to be gracious to us; but if we do not live generously, we are unable to receive the full benefits of his grace.

Why do people not give generously?
Largely this is down to a lack of trust in God and the fear of not having enough. It is greatly influenced by the prevailing attitudes of selfishness, greed and possessiveness that fill our society, expressed in the attitude of "looking after number one." This is a mindset that has affected many of us from which we need to break free. We have to question any outlook on life that goes against the generous nature of God.

The Spiritual Battle
Defeating fear, selfishness, and meanness is a spiritual battle. These are all features of 'demonic wisdom' (see James 3:15). We defeat this stronghold of the mind with the weapons of extravagant praise and thanksgiving, and acts of extreme generosity. We need to win the battle in the spirit and in the mind. Giving generously, and acting and speaking with real generosity can break things in the spirit realm.

An attitude of generosity leads to acts of generoslty
These acts will include forgiving others of which I have spoken of much throughout this book. Giving the benefit of the doubt to others is another expression of a generous heart. Thinking the best about other people and not taking offence, whether it is intended or not, are further expressions of a generous mindset. Serving others and going the extra mile are ways in which generosity is reflected, as well as in giving money.

We see so much of all this displayed in the life of Barnabas. He gave generously of his property (Acts 4:36-37). Later we find him giving the benefit of the doubt to Saul (Paul), and bringing him to the church when others were fearful and suspicious (Acts 9:26-27). It was Barnabas who went to Antioch where the Good News was first preached to Greeks. He did not show any misgiving about this new departure, but rejoiced in the fruit he witnessed (Acts 11:19-24). He even went the extra mile in going to Tarsus and searching out Saul to bring him to Antioch. Barnabas willingly sets off with Paul leaving his new home of Antioch behind in Acts 13. Finally, when Paul wants to send John Mark away, it is Barnabas who sees the best in the young man and takes him with him (Acts 15:36-41). Barnabas was known as a son of encouragement; he was also a father of generosity.

Our practical expressions of giving financially or in serving should of course be done in as hidden a manner as possible and never as an exhibition. Jesus made this very apparent in his teaching (see Matthew 6:1-4).

Here are some practical steps you can take to develop generous living:
1. Ask the Holy Spirit to show you anyone you need to forgive.
2. Regularly speak out forgiveness and blessing to those who wrong you.
3. Pray for anyone who in any way opposes you.

4. Be deliberate in being kind and generous in your attitude - in your workplace, while driving or anywhere else.
5. Give financially a bit more than what you might consider your dutiful giving.
6. Do something for someone that you in no way feel obliged to do.

So what does all this have to do with healing?
Proverbs 3:5-10 gives some clear guidelines on healthy and prosperous living.

Trust the LORD with all your heart
and lean not on your own understanding;
in all your ways acknowledge him'
and he will make your paths straight.
Do not be wise in your own eyes;
fear the LORD and shun evil.
This will bring health to your body
and nourishment to your bones.
Honour the LORD with your wealth,
with the firstfruits of all your crops;
then your barns will be filled to overflowing,
and your vats will brim over with new wine.

These verses indicate the value of trusting God and acknowledging his wisdom over our own. Alongside this, there is the summons to give of our wealth to the Lord. The consequences of following these admonitions are that we will experience direction, health and abundant provision. My experience has been that by honoring God first in our giving, Helen and I have known the amazing provision of God in so many ways over many years now. God is well able to look after us. We are called to be content in all circumstances whether with little or plenty. We have found the Lord always faithful.

One time when I was a student, we had virtually nothing. Helen prayed and asked the Father for £10 to feed the family. No-one else was there to hear that prayer. Later that day an envelope containing just a £10 note was put through our letterbox. That may not seem much, but it was what we needed and exactly what Helen asked for. That was just the first of many such incidences, like taking the car in for an unexpected repair, and the same morning receiving in the post a cheque for the same amount from someone we barely knew. We have generally asked God for what we have needed over the years. But one day Helen sensed the Lord tell her to ask him for £200. Not really needing that amount right then, Helen asked the Lord why she was to pray for this. His reply was that he is the God of more than enough. He is simply a generous Father. A cheque for £200 duly arrived in the post a couple of days later.

God knows what we need ahead of time and once again showed his provision for us in the following story. At the end of 1999, I left the pastoral ministry and stopped receiving any regular income. Helen and I felt to step out into the new ministry into which we knew God was leading us. At that time, Helen had a part-time job, working just a few hours a week, helping people with mental health problems. She loved doing this and received a small weekly wage. However, she felt she should be alongside me in the new ministry on a full-time basis. One evening as I was preaching in a church, Helen sat listening, and as she did, she prayed, asking God that if she were to give up her job then he would have to supply a cheque for £500. We arrived home late that evening to find an envelope from a friend waiting on us. It contained a cheque for £500! Helen actually dropped it on the floor in her excitement. The thing was, this friend later told us that he had the cheque ready to give us three weeks earlier, but he had influenza and this was the first time he had been able to get out to deliver the gift.

Trusting God that he is faithful, and recognising that his way is always right, leads us to give freely and receive freely the benefits of his gracious giving to us.

A second passage of Scripture that reveals a clear link between generosity and healing is Isaiah 58, as the following words from this chapter will make plain:

Is not this the kind of fasting I have chosen:
to loose the chains of injustice
and untie the cords of the yoke,
to set the oppressed free
and break every yoke?

Is it not to share your food with the hungry
and to provide the poor wanderer with shelter—
when you see the naked, to clothe him,
and not to turn away from your own flesh and
blood?

Then your light will break forth like the dawn,
*and **your healing will quickly appear;***
then your righteousness will go before you,
and the glory of the LORD will be your rear guard.

Then you will call, and the LORD will answer.
Isaiah 58:6-9a

There is a strong relation between how we treat people, especially the most needy and downtrodden, and how much healing we will see. How well has the Western church followed the injunctions of this portion of Scripture? Jesus declared that he was anointed to proclaim good news to the poor, or downtrodden, that is those who are up against it in life. It was in response to this passage of Scripture that our church first started going out taking food to and seeking to help homeless and needy people. That was also the setting where we started to see the miraculous works of God at a new level. Our Healing Room ministry in Glasgow has teams going out doing this every weekend. Stephen, who heads this up, sees God touching lives on the streets with great regularity.

A true spirit of generosity will be evidenced in giving to and caring for the disadvantaged around us. It is as we give away that we will receive, though we do not give out of that motivation. It is simply the way God has made life to work in his universal system.

Extreme generosity paves the way for the healing river to flow more fully and freely. As we live life this way, we discover the delight of being generous, and begin to abhor the meanness of spirit that once ruled us. The ministry of healing must always be practiced in this spirit of generosity.

Chapter 9
Stretch and Build

Enlarge the place of your tent,
stretch your tent curtains wide,
do not hold back;
lengthen your cords,
strengthen your stakes.
Isaiah 54:2

The river of God flows out in an ever-deepening way, bringing healing wherever it goes. The river stretches forth releasing his healing for the maladies and madness of this world. The church in this land has in many ways not flowed like the river. We have often under-achieved, working at much less than our full capacity in Christ, and not nearly reaching our potential in the power of the Holy Spirit.

God's call to his people has always been to be fruitful and multiply: from Adam to Abraham, Isaac and Jacob; and now to the church. He blesses us – affirms us and draws us into our potential – so that we can be a blessing. He is calling us to stretch and be stretched. He is challenging us to enlarge our tent.

This call, found in Isaiah 54, is made to a barren one. Why would someone without children need to enlarge their tent space? They would not unless they are about to burst forth and multiply. God often called the childless ones to get ready for expanse. To someone with many children it would be obvious that they might need more space. However, the barren one needs to believe the Word of God and act in faith. It is the response of faith that God is always looking for from his people.

Sing, Shout and See

The opening verse of Isaiah 54 calls the barren one to burst into song and to shout for joy. That takes real faith, believing God's word to us, rather than believing the circumstances we see with our natural eyes. Anyone can sing and shout when they are witnessing miracles and wonderful events. The test is whether we can respond to this word beforehand.

Isaiah 33:17 says, "Our eyes will see the king in his beauty and view a land that stretches afar."

This word was spoken to a people in captivity. Again, it is a word of hope and promise. God is calling us to see – and to see in a different manner. To see with eyes of faith that have been overlaid with the Spirit of revelation. We are to be enabled to see the King in his beauty. This is echoed in the New Testament, with John the Baptist's exhortation to his followers, to 'see the Lamb of God who takes away the sin of the world' (John 1:29). Then in Revelation 5:5, the angel encourages John the Apostle to 'see the Lion of the tribe of Judah who has triumphed.' We are to see Jesus in his sacrificial and triumphant beauty; the wonder of who he is, the Lord and Saviour. As we see and behold him, we are stretched forward by his compelling love and encompassing power, and begin to see the 'land that stretches afar.' Some Bible versions translate this as 'a far distant land.' Either way, God is calling us into something more and something that may now seem far away. It is not far off though, for Jesus is leading those who are willing into a fresh dynamic of life in his Spirit.

A Spacious Place

Isaac's servants went out to dig for water in the land (Genesis 26:17-25). Twice they discovered fresh water, only to have other herdsmen quarrel over it and dispute with them. They pressed on and dug another well, finding this time that no-one contested it. Therefore, Isaac named it 'Rehoboth', meaning room, for now he had room in the land and he would flourish. God leads us into spacious places, where we have room to stretch and grow. The enemy wants to hinder such growth, seeking to restrict us and hem us in. He attempts to set restrictive boundaries about what we can and cannot achieve. The Lord comes to remove the restrictions and re-set the boundary lines. It is really important who we let set the boundary lines in our lives.

I have observed how this has affected some of those who minister healing. A person can come with a back problem. We may have seen that sort of condition healed before, so there is no problem in believing for it again. This is within our boundary of faith. Then someone comes to us with terminal cancer, and the enemy tries to impose a boundary line that implies this is too much for us. As God leads us on in his river, he is forever extending the boundaries for us.

How are we to stretch and enlarge?
Stretch and enlarge as people: Physically we do this as we develop through childhood, and unfortunately, some of us continue to enlarge in some ways for too long! God wants to make us 'bigger people' in character. We have to go through many trials for this stretching of character to be worked in us.

He stretches us so that our capacity is increased. By this, I mean the capacity of our inner man to receive more of the Spirit and to produce more with the Spirit. We can be filled with the Spirit but not have the fullness of the Spirit. There is always more, and so we need to develop an increased capacity to receive the more he has for us. He wants to stretch and enlarge our mindsets concerning what is actually possible now, and not just in theory.

Stretch and enlarge in faith: Faith is a powerful substance. It will not break like some elastic band if it is stretched too far. It is a gift from God, but a gift we need to use and develop. It grows as it is exercised. Witnessing one miracle stretches our faith for the next one.

Our 'soup run' team took in a young woman late one night who had been addicted to heroin for several years. To 'pray her off' heroin was a mighty challenge to our faith, but we had seen God do other miracles through us. We had also read Jackie Pullinger's book *'Chasing the Dragon,'* and knew it could be done with the power of the Holy Spirit. After a week of being soaked in prayer and an atmosphere of worship to the Lord, the young woman was free, and remarkably had experienced no withdrawal symptoms. Any time she felt pain or unease, the team prayed over her in the Spirit and the problems went. Next time we would encounter the problem of drug addiction our faith boundary was set at a new level. (Of course, though God can deliver people from drugs this way, it still requires their full co-operation and a lot of aftercare).

Stretch and enlarge our 'tent': We need to get a bigger house! We literally had to do that a few years ago as we moved into my parents' home. We had to have an extension built to accommodate the seven of us (plus a dog) now living there.

Though you were ruined and made desolate and your land laid waste,
now you will be too small for your people,
and those who devoured you will be far away.
The children born in your bereavement will yet say in your hearing,
'This place is too small for us;
give us more space to live in.'
Isaiah 49:19-20

As the fruit of the harvest sweeps in to the church we may need some bigger buildings, but more importantly, we need life-giving ministries and structures to create space for people to grow in their new faith. I believe it is important we do not get weighed down with concerns for bricks and mortar, or become overly structured. We have been there too often and it has usually only hindered life. However, we do need to prepare ourselves for the fresh challenges of explosive growth.

Our 'tent' must not only be about people being gathered to us. It is in fact more about us spreading the influence of the Kingdom. This Kingdom influence needs to stretch across the land, for the nature of the Kingdom is that it spreads like yeast in the dough. We are to stretch the curtains of our tent wide, enveloping the most unlikely people and places, releasing the Kingdom as the compelling force of heaven.

Time to Build

As we stretch out and spread the fragrance of the Kingdom of God abroad in our land, it is essential that we learn to build. We need to occupy the land we take from the enemy. We need to learn to build without settling down. This is an apostolic work that keeps the right focus at all times. Some ministry gifts, like that of the evangelist, will want to stretch out, but rarely take time to establish and build. Others, like pastors and teachers, are good at building but do not always focus on stretching out. The apostolic gift is the one that incorporates a vision to stretch out and to build.

The apostle Paul was always reaching into new areas to spread the Gospel of the Kingdom. He was also concerned with building up the Body, and establishing the believers in the fullness of God. Much of the content of his letters is to do with building the church on the right foundations of truth in Christ.

Your people will rebuild the ancient ruins
and will raise up the age-old foundations;
you will be called Repairer of Broken Walls,
Restorer of Streets with Dwellings. Isaiah 58:12

God is about something in this day and he says that 'your people' or those from among you will do this – that is rebuild, raise up, repair, and restore. We do not need to wait on others coming from afar – we are to do this work. We are to set about rebuilding the ruins. Who has caused the ruins? We have, and the devil as we have empowered him. We are now to raise up the right foundations – Christ and his Word; apostles and prophets; mission and miracles; Spirit-led prayer and praise, and more.

First, God needs to undo the wrong foundations. He needs to 'ruin' us so he can build us in a new way (unless we are undone by God we will rebuild the old again instead of the new).

God is undoing us:
Isaiah cries out, "Woe is me, for I am undone!" (Isaiah 6:5 NKJV). We are ruined by the presence of God – undone by seeing the Lord. We are undone from false judgments, from pre-conceived ideas, presumptions, opinions, pride, and false humility; undone from our religiosity. God undoes us by encounters with him, not through fenced about religion, but raw encounters with his presence, where we are stripped of all pretence.

150

Undoing the devil's work: 1 John 3:8
The devil's work builds foundations of lies and fear, instead of truth, love and grace. We need to see the undoing of his interference: in the churches and in individual lives. The enemy tries to ruin us from being any use for God's Kingdom. God will ruin us so we can be of immense use in his Kingdom.

Once the wrong foundations are undone, and the rubble is cleared away, we can begin to raise up the right foundations and build the true temple of God. This will include, and indeed be preceded by a repairing of the walls like in Nehemiah's day. Other translations call this a 'repairing of the Breach,' that is the work of intercession or standing in the gap. It is prayer – yes, but more than prayer. It is a 'meeting' between what is on earth and what is in heaven, so that the gap (breach) between the two realities is brought closer together. That will always be bringing more of heaven's reality into earth's reality. Only as we repair this wall and keep it guarded, are we in position to complete the building work.

We build because God is a builder (see Hebrews 3:4; 11:10), and Jesus Christ is building his church (Matthew 16:18). We are his co-workers, and we are commanded to build. We are not building a material city, but something more enduring. We are building people: lives that were being ruined by sin, but are now being built into a spiritual house, to be a holy priesthood (1 Peter 2:5). We are to build people in Christ, and in faith, so that they overflow with his life (Colossians 2:6-7). We are building the church as a launching pad for further mission – that outward focus must always be maintained.

Paul warns us to be careful how we build (1 Corinthians 3:10). When the Israelites built an altar, they were not to use dressed stones or tools on it (Exodus 20:25). We need to be careful not to build with human understanding and means. 'Unless the LORD builds the house, its builders labour in vain' (Psalm 127:1). We must build on obedience to the words of Jesus:

Therefore everyone who hears these words of mine and puts them into practice is like a wise man who built his house on the rock Matthew 7:24.

It is not enough only to read or listen to the words of Jesus, good as that is; we build by living out his words in practice. Jesus is the cornerstone that sets everything in line, and the apostles and prophets are the foundations:

Consequently, you are no longer foreigners and aliens, but fellow citizens with God's people and members of God's household, built on the foundation of the apostles and prophets, with Christ Jesus himself as the chief cornerstone. In him the whole building is joined together and rises to become a holy temple in the Lord. And in him you too are being built together to become a dwelling in which God lives by his Spirit. Ephesians 2:19-22

What does the Scripture mean by the foundation of the apostles and prophets? Does this just refer to their writings in Scripture? I believe it also refers to apostolic and prophetic ministry, which is continuing today. Apostolic ministry is not neatly defined in the New Testament, but as I said before the apostolic keeps the right focus of reaching out and building up. This ministry breaks into new territory, and is accompanied by signs, wonders and miracles (Romans 15:17-20). It establishes and releases other ministries. The true apostolic gift needs to be recognised and allowed to function once again.

Alongside, and working together, is the prophetic gift. Of course, all God's people can prophesy as Acts 2:17-18 makes plain, but not all are prophets. Those with a genuine prophetic ministry will work under apostolic covering, complementing the apostolic work. Such prophets will stretch and build the Body of Christ. The gift of prophecy will stir up the Body to action, calling the church to go further than she has been before. Moreover, this gift will also encourage and edify the Body. The prophets will reveal what is on the heart of God, and see in the Spirit with a level of clarity; and the apostles will implement what God is saying, leading the church into new ground. These are the foundational ministries that will stretch, enlarge and build.

Finally in Isaiah 58:12 we are 'to restore streets to dwell in' – restoring true living conditions where there is no fear, no controlling, no stifling, but grace and truth are there, and life will flourish, and people will come into their full potential in Christ; they will be fully alive.

Conclusion: What time is it?

It is time to stretch our tent curtains wide and to build.

It is time to come out of any meanness of spirit and to live generously.

It is time to leave our disappointment behind and come into God's appointment to be fruitful.

It is time to abandon scepticism and doubt, and believe for a miraculous explosion.

It is time to stop hiding God's healing power in the church and start giving it away as a sign and a wonder.

It is time to move on from the shallow waters into the deeper things of God, so we can bring healing and release to the most damaged people.

It is time to cease from any grumbling and complaining, and work on creating conditions where healing grace can flow unhindered.

It is time to quit making excuses about our lack, and press in for the greater works of God's Kingdom.

It is time to be done with wavering between opinions and simply believe God.

It is time to release the healing power of Jesus Christ into our sick societies and a wounded world.

Appendix 1:
Overview of Healing in the Bible.

Having looked up and studied every mention of healing in the Bible I have put together this overview and classification of healing in the Scriptures. Of course, you could classify it differently and this list nowhere near contains or refers to every mention of healing.

What do we discover about healing in Scripture?
1. God is the LORD who heals – Exodus 15:26
2. All-inclusiveness of healing (affecting many types of illnesses) – Matthew 4:23-24; 9:35; 12:15; 15:30; Mark 1:34; Acts 5:16.
3. Healing is linked with God's presence – Ezekiel 47:12; Luke 5:17.
4. Healing is linked with the Word of God – Psalm 107:20; Matthew 8:8.
5. There is healing for the inner person – Psalm 147:3; Hebrews 12:12-13.
6. There is healing for mental illness – Daniel 4:34; Mark 5:1-20.
7. Healing is linked with forgiveness – Psalm 41:4; 103:3; Mark 2:1-12; James 5:16
8. People are healed when demons are cast out – Matthew 8:16; 12:22; 15:21-28; Mark 5:1-17; 9:14-27; Luke 6:18; 8:2; Acts 5:16; see also link in Matthew 10:1; Mark 6:13; and see also Luke 13:10-16; Acts 10:38.

9. Healing is linked with faith – Matthew 8:13; 9:27-31; 15:28; Mark 5:34; 10:46-52; Acts 14:9-10; Galatians 3:5; compare Mark 6:5.
10. Thankfulness is important in healing – Luke 17:15-19; Psalm 103:1-5.
11. Healing is linked with compassion – Matthew 14:14; Mark 1:40-42.
12. Healing leads to powerful evangelism – Matthew 10:5-8; Luke 9:1-6,11; 10:1-9; Acts 3:1-26; 4:29-31; 9:32-43
13. Healing is linked with intercession – Genesis 20:17; Numbers 12:13; 2 Chronicles 7:14: Acts 4:29-30; see also Acts 9:40; 28:8.
14. Spiritual gifts of healing – 1 Corinthians 12:9
15. The effect of words on health and for healing – Proverbs 12:18; 16:24
16. Healing of a nation/land – 2 Kings 2:19-22; 2 Chronicles 7:14; Psalm 60:2; Isaiah 30:26; Jeremiah 33:6; Revelation 22:2.

Modes of healing in Scripture:
1. Word of command – Mark 1:41; 7:34-35; Acts 9:34, 40; 14:10
2. Laying on of hands – Luke 4:40; Mark 6:5; Acts 28:8
3. Other touch – Matthew 8:15; Mark 7:31-37, also Mark 5:27-29
4. Oil – Mark 6:13; James 5:14
5. Saliva – Mark 7:33; 8:23
6. Handkerchief/apron – Acts 19:12
7. Water – 2 Kings 5:1-14
8. Salt – 2 Kings 2:19-22

Appendix 2:
God's Prescription for Health.

1. Living In freedom from sin and guilt – Psalm 103:3-5; Romans 8:1
2. Forgiving others, living free from bitterness – Matthew 6:12-14; Romans 12:17-21
3. Honouring of one's parents – Exodus 20:12, Ephesians 6:2-3
4. Trusting and resting in God's provision and faithfulness; being released from anxiety and stress – Proverbs 3:5-8; Hebrews 13:5-6
5. Hard work, recreation and rest in a right balance – Exodus 20:8-11
6. A mind filled with God's Word – Proverbs 4:20-27
7. The joy of the Lord – Nehemiah 8:10

Appendix 3:
Proverbs for Healing and Life:

3:5-8 Trust in the LORD with all your heart
    and lean not on your own understanding;
in all your ways acknowledge him,
    and he will make your paths straight.
Do not be wise in your own eyes;
    fear the LORD and shun evil.
This will bring health to your body
    and nourishment to your bones.

4:23 Above all else, guard your heart, for it is the
wellspring of life.

12:18 Reckless words pierce like a sword, but the
tongue of the wise brings healing.

12:25 An anxious heart weighs a man down, but a kind
word cheers him up.

13:12 Hope deferred makes the heart sick, but a
longing fulfilled is a tree of life

14:27 The fear of the LORD is a fountain of life.

14:30 A heart at peace gives life to the body, but envy
rots the bones

15:4 The tongue that brings healing is a tree of life, but
a deceitful tongue crushes the spirit

15:13 A happy heart makes the face cheerful, but heartache crushes the spirit

15:30 A cheerful look brings joy to the heart, and good news brings health to the bones

16:24 Pleasant words are a honeycomb, sweet to the soul and healing to the bones

17:22 A cheerful heart is good medicine, but a crushed spirit dries up the bones

18:14 A man's spirit sustains him in sickness, but a crushed spirit who can bear?

To find out more about the ministry of Healing Rooms look up the website of the International Association of Healing Rooms at www.healingrooms.com
To find out more about the ministry in Scotland go to www.healingrooms-scotland.com

To Contact the author:
Write to:
Healing Rooms Scotland
PO Box 7010
Glasgow
G76 7UL
U.K.

E-mail: admin@healingrooms-scotland.com